Development in Hindsight
The Economics of Common Sense

Development in Hindsight

The Economics of Common Sense

Peter de Haan

KIT Publishers – Amsterdam

Development in Hindsight; the Economics of Common Sense.
Peter de Haan

KIT Publishers
Mauritskade 63
P.O.Box 95001
1090 HA Amsterdam
The Netherlands
E-mail: publishers@kit.nl
www.kit.nl/publishers
www.landenreeks.nl

© 2006 KIT Publishers, the Netherlands

Editing: Ninette de Zylva, Arnhem, the Netherlands
Cover: Ronald Boiten, Amersfoort, the Netherlands
Design: Henny Scholten, Amsterdam, the Netherlands
Lay-out: Nadamo Bos, Driebergen, the Netherlands
Production: Meester en de Jonge, Lochem, the Netherlands

ISBN 90 6832 264 8
NUR 754

Contents

Foreword

The opportunity to write a foreword to a book of my staff does not come along every day. Peter de Haan has shown that he knows how to present difficult issues in an entertaining manner while raising contemporary development topics with the passion of a professional. I sincerely hope he reaches a broad audience of people involved in development world-wide.

The book focuses heavily on poverty, the core business of everyone in the field. As the author says in one of the essays, *The Institutional Dimension of Economic Growth*, poverty is a tragedy for many millions of poor women, men and children who have to fight every day just to survive. But poverty also threatens world peace and order without which no lasting solutions to the problem are possible. In the final analysis, poverty is an affront to civilization. These are the reasons why the Netherlands has long championed the cause of poverty eradication – the reasons which determine the focus of Dutch development assistance. Every year, the Netherlands contributes 0.8% of its GNP to this struggle – and to achieving the Millennium Development Goals. The Netherlands is one of the small number of donor countries – currently only five – that comply with the DAC 0.7% norm.

Peter de Haan is an economist by training, which explains the book's emphasis on economic growth as the most effective means of eradicating poverty. The first section sets out his views in five essays on themes such as globalization and the role of the state and the market in the development process. The second reproduces a series of articles he published in several Bolivian newspapers while assigned to the Royal Netherlands Embassy in La Paz. Most articles convey the message that poverty can be successfully attacked in Bolivia and the rest of the developing world only if the right mix of policies is applied and if there is solid political commitment to succeed.

Peter de Haan's book makes several very relevant suggestions for policymakers in both donor and aid-recipient countries. It is a must read for anyone working in the development field.

Agnes van Ardenne – van der Hoeven
Minister for Development Cooperation

Preface

This book contains a collection of essays and articles I wrote during the course of the past five years. When I came to Bolivia in September 2000, I had no intention whatsoever to write, but colleagues, friends, and the difficult – yet interesting – political climate in Bolivia spurred me on to do so.

It all started with Dr. Enrique García Ayaviri's suggestion of presenting a paper on economic growth to the Bolivian Academy of Economic Sciences. I accepted the invitation and the challenge and wrote my first essay: *The Institutional Dimension of Economic Growth*. That was not all. I had to present it in Spanish, which I did not speak well at the time, to a critical audience of accomplished Bolivian economists. I passed the test under great strain and to my complete surprise found myself accepted as a Visiting Academic of this distinguished Bolivian Institution. The other essays included in the first part of this book deal with the evolution of development economics, the role of the state and the market in the development process, including globalization and its effects on growth and poverty, as well as the question as to whether development assistance promotes growth.

The other challenge came from Wieck Wildeboer, our ambassador at the Netherlands Embassy in La Paz at the time. We were talking in February 2002 about the main issues of the coming Presidential elections in Bolivia, when all of a sudden the ambassador said: "Why don't you write down what we just discussed and try to have it published somewhere". This I did, and my then colleague Jorge Cortés – who had an enormous network amongst journalists – put me in touch with PULSO, a Bolivian weekly newspaper. To my complete surprise and infinite satisfaction they published the article and this is how my journalistic "career" began, which proved to be addictive. Six of the 15 articles I wrote for various Bolivian newspapers are included in the second part of this book.

Although writing can be tough and frustrating at times, one carries on for different reasons. George Orwell summarized them in all honesty and clarity in his wonderful piece *Why I Write*. For him there were various motives to write. He started by saying that "sheer egoism", the desire to seem clever, to be talked about, was a strong motive. According to Orwell, to pretend that this is not so is humbug. I agree, because seeing one's texts in print and receiving praise boosts one's ego. The second motive is aesthetic enthusiasm. Again I agree. The study of development economics provides the student with aesthetic pleasure. For instance, the neo-classical growth model and the subsequent improvements do indeed arouse aesthetic enthusiasm, at least that is what it did for me and this is what I want to share with the reader. The third motive is historical impulse, meaning finding true facts and presenting them to the reader for his judgment. To me the essay on *Globalization* does just that. A final motive is to share with the reader my thoughts on economic growth and development cooperation. Perhaps, this is the motive that radiates most strongly from the essays and articles. What we do as development workers may be necessary but it is certainly not sufficient, nor does it necessarily contribute to the promotion of growth and the eradication of poverty in poor countries.

I have been intrigued all my professional life by the factors that trigger growth. It has inspired me to discuss and read about this particular central issue of development, to enable us – the aid givers – to best help to promote growth and assist in the fight against poverty. I believe that too little attention has been paid to the promotion of private (and informal) sector development. Donor countries have been hypocritical in trade relations. High protection barriers still prevent many agricultural and other products from developing countries from entering our markets. Moreover, the conditions which we, donor countries, apply and which appeal to us, do not necessarily have equal relevance for recipient countries.

Finally, though we know that development aid alone cannot bring about economic growth and development, we often act as if it does. This is simply a sympathetic professional deformation, because most of us, aid workers, are very devoted to our mission.

Acknowledgements

Writing a book is not as lonely an undertaking as one might expect. Many colleagues, friends and family members were involved in reading the drafts, whose welcome comments and criticism greatly helped towards the improvement of my work.

I am deeply grateful for the support and generosity of: Lenny Ayala, Jorge Canelas, Asle Çetinel, Jorge Cortés, Juan de Dios Fernández, Alfonso García, Enrique García, Walter Guevara, Felipe Hartmann, Frederik Haver Droeze, Bert Helmsing, Alejandra Marquez, Juan Antonio Morales, Ron Muyzert, Jan Willem Nibbering, Malena Padilla, Robert Petri, Hans Ramaker, Mabel Ramon, Damaris Sanchez, Han-Maurits Schaapveld, Juan Cristóbal Soruco, Wim Spit, Wieck Wildeboer and Karina Zelaya.

Bruno Giussani helped me in particular to correct and make my writing more readable; he acted as a stimulating and intellectual sparring partner.

A very special word of thanks goes to my wife and life companion, Marisales Ramón, who not only patiently and critically reviewed all the texts, but also did an excellent job of translating some of them into Spanish.

Peter de Haan
La Paz, Bolivia
April 2006

Part I

Essays

Does development assistance promote growth?

Introduction

The other day I visited the office of the Canadian International Development Agency (CIDA) office in La Paz. There I saw an intriguing map on the wall: the world divided up into four colors. The color blue represented the world's oceans and the countries were colored yellow, orange or red, depicting their level of development. The yellow ones coincided with the rich OECD countries. The orange ones characterized the newly industrialized countries, such as China, India or Thailand, just to mention a few. The red ones, mainly in Sub-Saharan Africa, were the poor countries of the world. It showed the world map still littered with countries "in the red", so to speak, despite more than fifty years of development aid, thus prompting the question: Does aid promote economic growth?

This question keeps many researchers, policymakers, government officials, NGOs and politicians occupied, at both ends (donors and recipients) of the aid chain. The question is even more pertinent now that development assistance (including the G-8 inspired cancellation of poor developing countries' debts and the re-affirmation of achieving the eight Millennium Development Goals) is again high on the international political agenda.

The topic of the effectiveness of aid regularly pops up, almost in a cyclical manner. After the early optimism about aid effectiveness in the nineteen fifties and sixties, it became clear that the development of poor countries was not simply a question of filling up the *financing gap* (to break the vicious circle of poverty) until the time the aid receiving country would "take-off into self-sustained growth"[1]. Although this model has proved not to work, no other model of aid and growth has yet taken its place.

Sustained economic growth results were scarce[2]. The question thus arose as to whether or not the hypotheses on which international development assistance was founded were indeed valid. The less than inspiring results were, however, not the exclusive failure of aid. Most developing countries adopted policies that were inspired by the long and gloomy shadows cast by the Great Depression and the Second World War. New protectionist devices were applied on a wide scale by developed and developing countries alike. Furthermore, the collapse of world trade after October 1929 engendered a deep pessimism about export prospects of the Third World in the post-war years. Both influences led to autarkic models of development; many developing countries turned inward during the 1950s and the early 1960s, by introducing import-substituting industrialization behind protective walls. Only a few developing countries, such as South Korea, Taiwan, Hong Kong and Singapore, did not follow this course; instead they opted for an unorthodox outward-looking policy and all of them took-off spectacularly.

Aid in its proper perspective

From the outset it should be mentioned that the amounts of aid transferred annually are dwarfed by the flows of foreign direct investment (FDI) into developing countries[3]. Although aid may comprise a sizeable portion of the budget of some aid-receiving countries, aid *alone* cannot possibly finance economic development. Moreover, not all aid is directed at economic growth. Whether or not aid intended to promote growth does indeed do so, also depends on the development strategies of aid recipients, their own financial contribution, and – above all – on their policies and capacity to achieve sustained economic growth. And, lastly, it depends on the particular cultural setting within which development is to take place.

16

Methodologically it is, furthermore, difficult to isolate the contribution that aid makes to the economic growth of poor countries from other factors such as adverse climatic conditions, economic recessions, and changes in the international trade regime. There is also the element of the reliability and representativeness of the available statistical data.

Different points of view

There are different schools of thought on the question of aid effectiveness, one of which is based upon economic ideological grounds. One of the first and most prominent critics of the aid machinery was Peter Tamas Bauer. His *Dissent on Development* was published way back in 1971[4]. Deepak Lal also belongs to the original small group of critics. William Easterly joined the group later. Why I present dissenting rather than mainstream views is because of three reasons. First, my essay on the evolution of development economics (pp. 133-146) is about mainstream thinking. The second reason is that critics often provide an unorthodox and fresh perspective. Thirdly – and consequently – they stimulate the debate and broaden the views of all those involved in development, theoreticians and practitioners alike.

Another school of thought is empirically inspired. They let the data speak for themselves. The problem, however, is that some representatives of this school reach positive conclusions about the relationship between aid and economic growth, whilst others conclude rather negatively. Moreover, in cross-country regressions, one can never be sure whether they control all possible ways in which countries might differ.

Although we, aid workers, have the best intentions and generally work with zeal, none of us can deny that what we do may not always be the best or most appropriate contribution to economic growth. It is this uneasy feeling that inspired me to search the literature in an effort to find suggestions as to how aid can help promote growth more effectively.

Dissenting development economists

The thinking of development economics was long focused on state-led development: It was thought that governments had to play a prominent part in the development process. Those who questioned this *Dirigiste Dogma* were largely ignored for their politically incorrect thinking. Once socialism and central planning finally proved to be inappropriate for economic development, the dissenters gained respectability. I will briefly summarize the thinking of these critics: Peter Bauer, Deepak Lal and William Easterly.

Bauer's philosophy

Peter Bauer, who received the Milton Friedman Prize in 2000, applies classical economics to questions of poverty and development where conventional wisdom was hostile to market solutions for a very long time after World War II. Bauer belongs to that small group of dissenters who publicly resisted fashionable fads and fancies, yet influentially canvassed and consequently widely accepted[5]. Mainstream development thinking at the time was that benefiting well from incoming aid flows, recipient governments had to plan their economies and create new industries to substitute for foreign imports. And to give these nascent industries a chance, competition should be restricted through monopoly rights and barriers to foreign trade. Both theory and practice appalled Bauer, based on his experience with smallholdings in the Malaysian rubber industry and small-scale traders in West Africa. He became convinced that there could be wealth creation, even in subsistence economies, if only market forces were allowed to work.

Bauer started to develop alternative theories already in the 1960s. His argument, often put in a polemic style and seldom referring to empirical economists, went as follows. In the beginning all countries were poor. And if the vicious circle of poverty theory were true, mankind would still not "have come down from the trees". Throughout history countries had developed, not so much based on their natural resources but much more on ambition, resourcefulness, and effort. The concept of material progress, of steadily increasing control of man over his environment is Western, Bauer adds, and material progress depends on personal qualities, social institutions and mores, as well as political arrangements which make for endeavor and achievement. In this sense, Bauer states that cultures of large parts of the less developed world are uncongenial to economic achievement and advance[6].

Bauer maintains that the idea of the vicious circle has been a major lapse in modern development economics. It has influenced policy (i.e., the financing gap) considerably. It was a major element in the advocacy of massive state economic controls on the ground that only drastic policies of resource mobilization would enable an economy to break the vicious circle. It was also a major strand in the successful advocacy of government-to-government subsidies in the form of foreign aid[7]. Ironically, Bauer says that there would not be the concept of Third World if it were not for the invention of foreign aid. Opportunities for private profit hold the key to development, according to Bauer, and not government plans. Governments had the limited – though crucial – role of protecting property rights, enforcing contracts, treating everybody equally before the law, minimizing inflation and keeping taxes low. In practice, most poor country governments have neglected this role: aid politicized economies, putting money into the hands of governments instead of profitable business.

Foreign aid is also inspired by an erroneous guilt felt by Western aid-giving countries. Guilt, says Bauer, is a prerogative of the West. The conviction is that the West gained its richness at the expense of poor Third World countries. In this vein the poor are considered passive but virtuous, the rich as active but wicked. Bauer's response is that incomes whether of the rich or of the poor are earned by their recipients, and are not extracted from the poor. Bauer adds that many of the African and Asian colonies progressed very rapidly during colonial rule and much more so than the independent countries in the same area.

Aid increased the patronage and power of recipient governments pursuing policies that stifled entrepreneurship and market forces. The key is that aid should help to create the right conditions for markets to flourish. Bauer concludes that foreign aid is demonstrably neither necessary nor sufficient to promote economic progress in the Third World. It is much more likely to inhibit economic advance than to promote it.

Bauer was also controversial in opposing policies to reduce income inequality. This is not because he favors inequality, but because policies designed to promote equality usually infringe personal liberties to such an extent as to slow economic development. As Amartya Sen concluded in his introduction to Bauer's *From Subsistence to Exchange*, what Bauer said has become a part of the new establishment of ideas, although most aid is still government to government.

Lal and the Dirigiste Dogma

Lal concentrates his critique on the dirigiste dogma. What are the elements of this dogma? In Lal's own words: "The major one is the belief that the price mechanism, or the working of a market economy, needs to be supplanted by various forms of direct government control, both national and international, to promote economic development... The essential task of government is seen as charting and implementing a 'strategy' for rapid and equitable growth that attaches prime importance to macro-economic aggregates... The third element is the belief that the classical 19th century liberal case for free trade is invalid for developing countries, and thus government restriction of international trade and payments is necessary for development. Finally, it is believed that, to alleviate poverty and improve domestic income distribution, massive and continuing government intervention is required to re-distribute assets and to manipulate the returns of different types of labor and capital through pervasive price and (if possible) wage controls"[8].

Lal is not a laissez faire economist, neither is he against state intervention. The central issue of state intervention is its form and extent, and not its complete absence, as maintained by the dirigists in their critique of classical economics. Lal shares the dirigist objectives, i.e., rapid and equitable economic growth. However, he disagrees with the approach taken by them, which he finds dubious.

His arguments are as follows. Traditional development economists say that developing countries are unequal partners in the world trading and payment system; hence, the rules of the game of the liberal international economic order must be changed to serve the interests of developing countries. Lal notes that the analytical and empirical bases of development economics were provided by Keynesian thinking and by the experience of developing countries during the Great Depression. Both the central theoretical concern of Keynesian economics – the determinants of the level of economic activity rather than the relative prices of commodities and factors of production – and its distinctive method – national income-expenditure analysis – were adopted by development economists. The allocation of given resources, a major concern of classical economics, was considered of minor importance. This thinking implied a rejection of the primary role of changes in relative prices in the mediation of imbalances in the supply and demand for different commodities. According to the Keynesian philosophy, changes in income were substituted as the major adjustment mechanism to address these imbalances. As a result, the neglect of the price mechanism is almost built into macro-economic thinking and in development planning.

Lal points to another neglect of development economics: that it does not take into account the contribution of welfare economics. This is odd, as welfare economics provides the reasons why a real world laissez faire economy is not likely to be Pareto-efficient, because (i) it is unlikely to be perfectly competitive, and (ii) it will certainly lack universal markets. Thus there would seem to be a case for government intervention anyway. It would be carrying the argument too far to jump to the conclusion that because laissez-faire may be inefficient and inequitable, any form of government intervention would entail a welfare improvement. The most serious current distortions in many developing countries, says Lal, are not those flowing from the inevitable imperfections of the market but from policy-induced, and thus far from inevitable, distortions created by irrational *dirigisme*.

As for foreign aid, Lal's opinion is not much different from that of Bauer. Yet, I would say that it has a bit more nuance. Lal agrees with Bauer that the fundamental case for giving aid is a moral issue, i.e., that the rich should help the poor. Based on this, many Third World spokesmen, including their ideological friends in the rich countries, have sought to infer a would-be existence of an international society that subscribes to an egalitarian morality from which the right of the poor to be aided by the rich can be deduced. Aid is then demanded as a matter of right and not as a charitable handout. But since there is no such international society, no such right can be established. The problem for rich countries willing to help fight poverty via government-to-government aid is that outsiders cannot question the relationship that a sovereign recipient government has with its poor population. Thus, concludes Lal, there is a strict limitation on the donors' ability to ensure that they are helping the poor. If aid to poor countries is substantial, as is the case in many Sub-Saharan African countries, these countries have the tendency to depend entirely on handouts and start behaving as paupers.

The leverage that donors can exercise to influence the policies of Third World governments through financial assistance is limited. After all, domestic economic management matters more than foreign financial aid. Lal makes an exception for technical advice. This, in some instances, may have had an appreciable effect in making public policies more economically rational. He concludes by saying that aid can be of importance if ideas have an influence on the conduct of public affairs. He points to successful policy reforms in Taiwan, South Korea, and India[9].

Easterly and the cartel of good intentions

William Easterly, former World Bank economist, is the third dissenter presented here. His magnum opus so far is the *Elusive Quest for Growth*, although publishing this impressive and honest account about his thinking on aid theories and hands-on experience in development work did cost him his job at the Bank[10]. Easterly is now professor of the economics faculty at New York University and he is associated with the think tank Center for Global Development, as well as with the Institute for International Development.

Easterly's central theme is that economists have too often provided formulas for economic development that violated the basic principle of economics. That basic principle simply is what a wise old person once told him: "People do what they get paid to do; what they don't get paid to do, they won't do"[11]. The magic word is incentives, in that people, businesses, government employees, and even donors respond to incentives.

Development economists have studied the question of how economic growth responds to incentives. These incentives can work in two ways: positive or negative. They may lead economic actors in opposite directions and in many developing countries the incentive structure often drives these actors into the wrong direction[12]. Incentives for donors should be their contribution to economic growth of poor countries, or more fashionably, to help eradicate poverty. Both are very hard to measure and hard to achieve. Hence, there is the tendency to emphasize money disbursed as an indication of success. Incentives are thus geared to moving money and pushing loans[13]. Recipient governments may have little incentive to raise the productive potential of their poor population, especially when doing so might engender political activism that would threaten the current political elite. Easterly concludes that if we ensure that the donor community, the governments of poor countries and their citizens all have the right incentives, development will happen.

Thus far, the quest for growth has been elusive for two reasons, says Easterly. First, successive aid-growth theories proved to be inadequate, in the sense that they not only failed to explain past growth but also failed to predict future growth. Second, development aid policies and practices did not contribute to sustained economic growth of poor countries.

Regarding the theoretical underpinning of aid, Easterly refutes the double financing gap model. Also other theories, such as Rostow's five stages model, the neo-classical and the endogenous growth models, proved not to work in practice[14]. Yet, the financing gap model is still being applied by various aid agencies. Easterly concludes that so far no other theoretical model has substituted previous ones. He doubts whether it is possible at all to come up with an aid-growth model that would be universally applicable, as poor nations include a very wide variety of cultures, institutions and histories. He says: "The idea of aggregating all this diversity into a 'developing world' that will 'take off' with foreign aid is a heroic simplification"[15].

Easterly is rather merciless regarding aid in the disguise of the cartel of good intentions. He says that aid agencies define their output as money disbursed rather than effective services delivered. They engage in spin control, hiding the fact that they learned little from past failures, and they put enormous demands on scarce administrative capacity in poor countries[16]. The aid bureaucracy is functioning on the wrong, perverse, incentives because, amongst others, of a lack of (critical) feedback from beneficiaries, and of competitive pressure from other aid agencies; hence the cartel of good intentions.

In concluding, Easterly shares with us disturbing messages, though he is not as cynical about development aid as Bauer, for example. He starts his *Elusive Quest for Growth* with a compassionate plea for continued support to poor countries: The gaping differences in the lives of the poor and the rich supply his motivation to press on with his quest. Easterly concludes that nothing would be sadder than to give up the quest for growth altogether.

The empiricists

A large and widening crowd of development economists is trying to figure out, by way of statistical means, what the contribution of aid to economic growth has been. Since the introduction of the Poverty Reduction Strategies and the Millennium Development Goals, the question as to what extent aid and growth could contribute to the fight against poverty has been added[17].

Once one tries to review the literature, one is overwhelmed by the sheer quantity of studies that have seen the light since the invention of development assistance. A useful overview, in historical perspective, is provided by Clemens, Radelet, and Bhavnani in: *Counting Chickens When they Hatch: The Short-Term Effect of Aid on Growth*[18]. The authors distinguish four phases in the "unfinished business in 30 years of research", as they put it.

The earliest attempts, preceding these phases, were built on growth models like those of Harrrod-Domar and Rostow. These studies, however, did not attempt to measure the aid-growth relationship.

Four phases

The first phase, according to Clemens et al. really started in 1970 with an "opening salvo" by Keith Griffin, in reaction to the earlier hypothesis that foreign aid had to fill the financing gap. Griffin concludes that it is quite possible that the slight positive effect of foreign capital in raising investment will be more offset by a decline in the output-capital ratio, so that the growth rate actually falls[19].

Papanek launched the second phase [20]. He separated aid from other types of foreign capital and became the first researcher to correlate growth and aid. He found a strongly significant positive correlation between aid and growth in 51 countries during three five-year periods over 1950-1965. Unfortunately, this result is not statistically significant because he restricted the sample to the Americas.

Mosley started the third phase. He addressed the direction of causality between aid and growth. He found a negative but insignificant effect of aid on growth over the period 1970-1977 in an 83-country cross-section[21]. However, as Mosley and others admit, the data deserve further exploration.

Controversy

The rest of the third phase is a period of controversies. There are researchers who claim a positive and significant effect of aid on growth. But others do not find such a positive effect[22]. These conclusions, which are at great variance, may be the result of the application of different definitions of aid, a difference in clusters of time periods taken, different quantities and types of developing countries included in the samples, and so forth.

Peter Boone's article *Politics and the effectiveness of foreign aid*, published in 1996, concluded that aid programs have not engendered or correlated with the basic ingredients that cause growth[23]. He found that aid financed consumption rather than investment. Many researchers have taken his findings as a confirmation of the so-called "macro-micro paradox", i.e., that many aid-funded projects show micro-level positive returns that are undetectable at the macro-level.

Fourth phase

And it is at that point that the fourth phase begins, during which the literature splits into two strands: one trying to explain the paradox and the other denying its existence. The former, conditional, strand confirms that the average effect of aid across all countries is indeed roughly zero, and in only some countries the relationship is positive at times. The general objective of this strand's literature was to find out why aid is not effective in the typical recipient country, while it could be effective in others. As for the latter, Burnside and Dollar's article *Aid, Policies and Growth*[24] did demonstrate that aid could indeed be effective in recipient countries endowed with better development policies and stronger institutions[25]. This article had a major influence on the donor community, in that aid became more selective in favoring poor countries with these particular characteristics.

The ones denying the macro-micro paradox belong to the *unconditional* variety, so to speak. They say that Boone is wrong. What they maintain instead is that although aid does not have the same effect everywhere, aid *does* on average have a positive growth impact. Researchers of this strand argue that Boone's assumptions of a linear impact of aid on growth is less realistic than a non-linear relationship between the two, in which aid is subject to "diminishing returns", as there is some limit to recipients' capacity to absorb more aid.

Hansen and Tarp demonstrate in *Aid and Growth Regressions*[26] that aid increases the growth rate. However, they note that the estimated effectiveness of aid is highly sensitive to the choice of the estimator and the set of control variables. The authors also conclude that when investment and human capital are controlled, no positive effect of aid could be registered. Yet, aid continues to impact on growth via investment, contrary to what Easterly says about this relationship. Hansen and Tarp warn, however, that aid's impact on growth via investment requires better theoretical explanations, before one can derive satisfactory empirical specifications and formulate useful testable hypotheses[27].

Clemens et al. present a third reaction to Boone's article, focusing on matching aid flows to a realistic time period over which these aid flows might influence growth. Earlier research applied time periods of 4 to 5 years. But if the period chosen was ten or more years, the coefficient of instrumented aid would have turned out to be positive. Another very interesting aspect that Clemens et al. introduce is the following. They investigate the short-run impact of that part of aid whose effects on growth can reasonably be expected in the short-run. As far as I know, this is the first time aid is disaggregated, and with reason. After all, all foreign aid is not the same: there is technical assistance, there is investment in health and education, there is aid in infrastructure, humanitarian and emergency aid, and there is general budget support, just to mention the most common forms. All of them have different objectives and thus a different impact.

What Clemens et al. have done is to select those forms of aid that may have an impact on economic growth in the short-run[28]. This short-impact aid is defined as an aid disbursement that can plausibly raise GDP per capita to a permanently higher level within roughly four years. The four-year period had been chosen to conform to the time periods chosen by most of the recent aid-growth studies. In broad terms, short-impact aid is (i) budget support or program aid given for any purpose, (ii) project aid given for real sector investments for infrastructure or to directly support production in transportation, communications, energy, banking, agriculture and industry. This type of aid accounts for 53% of all aid flows.

Clemens et al. see a positive, causal relationship between this short-term impact aid and economic growth, be it with diminishing returns. USD 1 increase in short-term impact aid, will raise output (and income) by USD 1.64 in present value in the typical recipient country, thanks to its multiplier effect. Contrary to Burnside and Dollar's observation, this result does not depend on a recipient's level of income or quality of its institutions and policies. Clemens et al. found that short-term impact aid causes growth, on average, *regardless* of these characteristics[29]. They admit though that the impact on growth is somewhat larger in countries with more open trade, lower inflation, lower budget deficits, and which effectively battle corruption, guard property rights, and cultivate a respect for law. But the critical reader may ask: what about Africa's dismal growth performance? The authors' response is that the average growth in Sub-Saharan Africa was *minus* 0.23%, but it would have been 0.57% lower had the region not received more than the average percentage of aid. In other words, aid prevented Sub-Saharan Africa from sinking deeper in the mud.

Burnside and Dollar revisited

As already noted, Burnside and Dollar's article was welcomed with open arms by the donor community as it suggested that aid *does* promote growth; and donors – of course – like to hear that what they do is effective. Their article had a large influence on donor attitudes in that they shifted their assistance to those developing countries with better policies and institutions, leaving the basket case countries and failed states more and more on their own.

Burnside and Dollar's (B&D) article consists of a number of regressions in which the dependent variable of growth rates in developing countries depends on initial per capita national income, an index that measures institutional and policy distortions, foreign aid and aid interacted with policies. Their article triggered many reactions, amongst others, from Easterly, Levine and Roodman. Their reaction *New Data, New Doubts: A Comment on Burnside and Dollar's "Aid, Policies and Growth"*, includes a data-gathering exercise that (i) updates B&D's data from 1970-1993 to 1970-1997, (ii) includes more countries, and (iii) fills in missing data for the original period[30]. Their conclusion is that B&D's finding is *not* robust to the use of these additional data. The authors note, however, that their paper does not argue that aid is ineffective. They make a much more limited claim. They simply say that adding additional data to the B&D study of aid effectiveness raises new doubts about its effectiveness, and suggest that economists and policymakers should be less positive about concluding that foreign aid will boost growth in countries with good policies and ditto institutions. However, Easterly et al. conclude that B&D's article is not yet the final answer on this critical issue.

All reactions to their first article prompted B&D to update their study, which they did in 2004, applying a new data set focusing on the 1990s[31]. They now find that in the 1990s the allocation of aid to low-income countries favored ones with better institutional quality. The evidence supports, moreover, that the impact of aid indeed depends on the quality of state institutions and policies. The interaction between aid and institutional quality has a robust positive relationship with growth. B&D also conclude that there is no support for the competing hypothesis that aid has the same positive effect everywhere; a conclusion that Clemens et al. had already drawn.

IMF working papers

William Easterly once said that growth regressions were like firearms, it is dangerous to leave them lying around. This may have prompted two IMF economists to have them analyzed once again. And this is what Rajan and Subramanian did[32]. Their objective was to present, in one place and using one framework, results on the different aspects of the aid-growth relationship and to do so both in cross-section and panel contexts.

They added two aspects to the already voluminous literature on aid effectiveness. First, they isolated the exogenous component of aid. Their reasoning was that aid may go to different recipient countries for different reasons: aid may go to countries in response to a natural disaster – which would explain a negative correlation; but aid may also be directed to countries who have used it well in the past – implying a positive correlation. They also tested the general validity of the aid-growth relationship. Within one framework, they tested the robustness of the relationship across time horizons (medium and long run) and periods (1960s through 1990s), sources of aid (multilateral and bilateral), types of aid (economic, social, food, etc.), timing of impact of aid, specifications (cross-section and panel), and samples. The authors' purpose was to answer the question: even though the cross-country regression framework is flawed, what does it *really* say about the impact of aid on growth?

Rajan and Subramanian (R&S) find little evidence of a robust positive impact of aid on growth. They also find no evidence that aid works more effectively in better policy, institutional, or geographical environments, or that certain kinds of aid work better than others; this last-mentioned aspect is explained by aid's high degree of fungibility. R&S thus refute what Burnside and Dollar found. Their conclusions also refute the positive short-term aid effect on growth as presented by Clemens et al.

R&S's findings obviously relate to the past and therefore do not imply that aid may not be effective in the future. The authors conclude that the aid apparatus will have to be rethought, if aid were to be more effective. R&S then ask themselves what aspects of aid would offset the would-be indisputable growth enhancing effects of resource transfers. They conclude that in dealing with this intriguing question, one has to move away from the traditional cross-sectional analysis and focus on direct evidence of the channels through which aid might help or hinder growth. They have done so and published their results in *What Undermines Aid's Impact on Growth?*[33].

R&S talk of aid inflows having systematic adverse effects on a country's competitiveness, as reflected in a decline in the share of labor-intensive and tradable industries in the manufacturing sector. They explain this phenomenon through the influence of aid flows on exchange rate overvaluation, otherwise known as the Dutch Disease. What they say is that in a flexible exchange regime aid inflows push up the nominal exchange rate, which make the prices of the traded goods sector uncompetitive if the wages in that sector would not be adjusted downwards. In a situation of fixed exchange rates, aid inflows spent on domestic goods will push up the price of other critical resources that are in limited supply. This would render uncompetitive those industries that depend on these resources and face international competition. Aid, by contrast, might even increase if exchange rate overvaluation leads to poor economic performance, thus further exacerbating the problem. The good news is that remittances by migrants to their home countries do not have these adverse effects. What R&S did not include in their methodology, is the influence of foreign direct investment, nor the influence of other capital inflows.

The authors were very careful not to jump to negative conclusions. What they say is that at the very least their work suggests that poor countries may not have the absorptive capacity to take in massive quantities of aid up front without it creating substantial adverse effects on that country's export competitiveness. It would be far better for them to build up a larger body of skilled workers, but this takes time. A good solution might be, according to R&S, to start slowly but to accelerate as capacity builds up. Even though the world is impatient for the poor to develop, development – especially when expected from the outside – does require patience.

What can we learn from the empiricists?

The large variety of econometric analyses offers contradictory conclusions. As for the effectiveness of aid to promote growth, the jury is still out, so to speak. However, on the basis of the studies, an unjustified conclusion would be that aid is not effective in the promotion of economic growth of poor countries. On the other hand, one cannot also conclude that aid has been effective in helping the majority of poor countries to "take off".

A note of caution is called for here. Measuring the relationship between aid and growth by way of econometric techniques has its limits. Almost all analyses hinge on the statistical significance of variables in cross-country regressions involving aid. Roodman notes that most test results are fragile. All of them embody a set of choices concerning model specification and data[34]. Yet, we should not entirely dismiss their results, nor should we jump to general conclusions. Roodman asks himself why analyses of aid effectiveness "...do not shine more clearly through the numbers?"[35]. There are several reasons. Aid is not a decisive factor for development, at least not as important as high quality schooling, domestic savings and investment or the quality of governance, for example. As we have seen, aid is not homogenous, meaning that not all aid is directed to promote economic growth. Finally, aid can be used poorly. Even if some studies indicate a positive effect of aid on growth, then the question for the policymakers remains as to where aid should be sent and in what forms.

Suggestions for improvement

I started this essay by saying that I was curious to find out what the literature could offer by way of suggestions to improve aid delivery in the pursuit of economic growth. I cannot say that I am impressed with what I found. The suggestions are of a rather general nature. Here are some.

Easterly, concluding that the bureaucratic way of delivery of foreign aid has been unsatisfactory, suggests exploring the possibility of providing cash grants to the poor, vouchers for public services given to poor communities, and transferring aid funds through NGOs, as well as contracting out aid services to private firms[36]. Most of the suggestions are already being applied. It would be interesting to learn about the pros and cons of these alternative delivery systems, and in which particular circumstances they are likely to work.

Incentives is Easterly's central theme in *The Elusive Quest for Growth*. He rightly notes that it is devilishly difficult to get incentives right for creating growth. This happens, for instance, when government incentives induce technological adaptation, high-quality investment in machines, and high-quality schooling. This is fine, but Easterly depicts an almost ideal (third) world. However, the reality is much closer to what Douglass North sketched, in that the typical poor country has no incentives to create efficient economic rules (refer to footnote 12). As for the donors, as long as their internal incentive structure is still favoring disbursements instead of the achievement of results in the field, we are a long way off from improved service delivery of aid agencies. The efforts to better harmonize and align are laudable, but they do not take away the deeper lying causes of the perverse and counterproductive aspects of the aid machinery.

Birdsall, Rodrik and Subramanian present some suggestions in *How to Help Poor Countries*[37]. They note that there is a healthy move away from dispensing aid up-front in the expectation that results be achieved, to providing aid based on the achievement of pre-agreed benchmarks of progress. This is a good move, because it rewards recipients for results achieved, and it is a good example of Easterly's suggestion of providing the right incentives.

Another suggestion is to allot enough emission rights to poor countries to ensure their future growth. Market-based trading guarantees that pollution would be cut where costs are lowest. For example: if costs are lower in India than in the US, then the US could pay India to pollute less, and India would be financially better off for doing so. Various donors, including the Netherlands, are already putting this model into practice.

Other positive actions would be: (i) that rich countries take steps against corrupt leaders of poor countries; (ii) assisting in research and development; and (iii) enhancing global labor mobility. Corrupt leaders of poor countries should be put on a black list. Companies that deal with regimes on that black list would risk losing their claims to repayment if, at a later date, a lawful government decided to default on the debt passed down by its unlawful predecessor.

Donor countries can also spur technological advances that serve the interests of poor countries, so as to break a Catch 22 situation: developing countries remain poor because of limited technological opportunities, while these opportunities remain difficult to create precisely because the countries are poor. The Bill & Melinda Gates Foundation, for example, is pouring investments into researching treatments of tropical diseases and aids to benefit patients precisely in poor countries. Another possibility would be that rich countries would financially reward (via guaranteed purchase agreements) the development of new technologies specifically beneficial to poor countries. To my mind, the authors' proposal to promote global skilled and unskilled labor mobility is naive. Under their plan the workers from poor countries would be allowed to work for three to five years in rich countries, after which they would go home again and use their savings to invest there. Practice, however, shows that they do not want to return to their home countries for lack of opportunities; they just stay put and their children then become second-generation immigrants.

The World Bank's Learning Curve

I wrote the suggestions above before I came across the World Bank's *Economic Growth in the 1990s: Learning from a Decade of Reform*[38]. Friend and foe agree that this is a remarkable report. The Bank cannot be blamed for being static and for not accepting the facts of development. Noteworthy is that the report bids farewell to the Washington Consensus, as it did not live up to its high growth and poverty alleviation expectations. The report confirms that a one size fits all policy has not worked, as each developing country is unique in its political, institutional and economic composition.

The report concludes with the idea that gains in growth would be won entirely through policy improvements was unrealistic. Policy decisions taken in the pursuit of efficiency gains were mistaken for growth strategies. The report points to the fact that the reforms of the past decade did not focus on the binding constraints to economic growth of aid receiving countries. However, removing obstacles that make growth impossible may not be enough: growth-oriented action in the domain of, for example, technological catch-up, and encouragement of private and public risk taking may be needed as well. The focus should be on identifying *the* constraints that prevent economic growth of a particular country from taking off – and sustaining it – through the right sequence of policies needed in each situation.

Those developing countries that provide positive experiences high-light the importance of the investment climate and of providing predictable conditions for investors. Also common to all successes is that four conditions have been fulfilled: rapid accumulation of capital, efficient resource allocation, technological progress, and sharing of the benefits of growth. Yet, each successful country achieved them in their own specific way.

Economic Growth in the 1990s concludes by stating that: "...analytical work needs to change its orientation, away from seeking to assess how far policies diverge from optimality, to seeking to assess what policy and institutional conditions – for capital accumulation, shared growth, productivity growth, and risk taking in a country-specific context – are needed to set the growth process in motion"[39].

For research this would mean that the focus of growth strategies and development assistance has to be rethought. Up to now the focus has been on the nation-state with the implicit assumption that developing countries per capita incomes will converge with those of the industrialized ones. There is now evidence that this assumption does not always hold. Convergence is less a force now than anticipated in the past. Moreover, within countries income differences across regions are as large as income differences across countries. This implies that more attention should be paid to the forces driving agglomeration and migration, both within and across countries.

As for "behavior", as the report put it, all this means is that more humility should be applied than in the past, and more openness in the range of solutions possible, as well as more empathy with the specific country's perspectives.

Rodrik's inspiration

Dani Rodrik can claim that his thinking greatly influenced the central message of *Economic Growth in the 1990s*. He already wrote about growth strategies, emphasizing the phenomenon of binding constraints since the early years of this century[40]. His most recent article, entitled *Goodbye Washington Consensus, Hello Washington Confusion?*[41], clearly explains why Rodrik believes that overcoming the binding constraints of economic growth may be the best way forward, perhaps because, as Rodrik admits, economic science is still unfalsifiable.

In the past, says Rodrik, too little attention was paid to stimulating the dynamic forces that lie behind the growth process. And different contexts require different solutions to solving problems. Enhancing private investment incentives may require improving the security of property rights in one country, but enhancing the financial sector in another. This explains why successful growth countries, such as Bangladesh, Botswana, Chile, China, Egypt and India, have such diverse policy configurations. It also explains why attempts to copy successful policy reforms of one country in another often end up in failure.

Rodrik distances himself somewhat, and so does *Economic Growth in the 1990s*, from the importance accorded to institutions in the growth process, based upon two considerations. First, the cross-national literature has been unable to establish a strong causal link between any particular design feature of institutions and economic growth. Second, when institutional indicators are introduced in growth regressions, the link is weak and not robust. Moreover, empirical work focusing on transitions into and out of growth has found little evidence that large-scale institutional transformations play a role. Rodrik cites the example of India's transition to high growth in the early 1980s, which was preceded by no identifiable institutional change. This and other growth experiences suggest that policymakers interested in igniting growth may be better served by targeting the most binding constraints of economic growth, rather than by investing scarce political and administrative capital on ambitious institutional reforms. Rodrik admits that institutional reform will be needed eventually to sustain economic growth, but it may be easier and more effective to do that when the economy is already growing[42].

Rodrik ends his article with a practical guide for formulating growth strategies. First, a country-specific diagnostic should be undertaken to figure out where the most significant constraints to economic growth would be. Second, an imaginative policy design should be formulated to precisely target the identified constraints. And third, the process of diagnosis and policy response should be institutionalized so as to ensure that the economy remains dynamic and growth does not fizzle out, which is so often the case in the typical developing country.

Hausmann, Rodrik and Velasco developed a framework that intends to help identify the most binding constraints[43]. The central theme of this framework is that in a low-income country, economic activity must be constrained by at least one of the following factors: (i) either the cost of finance must be too high, or (ii) the private return to investment must be low. Once one of these two has been identified as being the most binding, the framework provides further possibilities that may explain why the economy does not take off. Once the constraints have been identified they will serve as a solid basis for policy reform and allow donors to know what to invest in and what not. If, for instance, human capital were a serious constraint, one would expect investments in education to have comparatively high returns. It would thus make sense (also for donors) to invest in appropriate education. As for policy design, this should be focused on market failures, and the policies should be as close as possible to the source of the distortion.

The reforms resulting from this exercise should be institutionalized because the nature of the binding constraints will change over time, and everything should be done to prevent growth from fizzling out. What is needed to sustain growth is the maintaining of productive dynamism, through diversification into new areas of tradable goods and services, for instance. Second, domestic institutions should be strengthened to better withstand external shocks, as the most frequent collapse in growth is the inability to deal with them. Aid could greatly help mitigate these shocks. Alas, aid delivery is not yet responsive to these shocks. Collier and Dehn, for instance, conclude that should donors take these shocks into account in their allocation rules, the effectiveness of aid can be expected to increase[44]. As for the Washington Confusion in the title of Rodrik's article, this refers to the unwavering stance of the IMF regarding required reforms that would trigger economic growth. The IMF is still of the opinion that the reforms as advocated by the Washington Consensus were not deep and far enough to result in beneficial growth and poverty alleviation. The failures were caused by too little reform of the kind that Washington has advocated, and not the nature of these reforms itself. Rodrik concludes in the context of the differing opinions in Washington, that the standard policy reforms did not produce lasting effects where background institutional conditions were poor; hence, a minimum institutional framework would be required.

Some observations

Before drawing a few conclusions, the development experiences over the past half-century merit some observations. Thus far, more than fifty years of aid has not resulted in putting the majority of poor countries on the path of economic growth. Surely, there are exceptions such as Botswana, Chile and Mauritius, and quite a few South and South-East Asian countries. They all prove that it can be done. Indeed, most poor countries did demonstrate bouts of growth but many failed to sustain them. Out of 110 countries analyzed in a sample by Hausmann, Pritchett and Rodrik, 60 (including quite a few African countries) have had at least one occurrence of rapid growth, suggesting that achieving rapid growth over the medium term is not something that is tremendously difficult to achieve[45]. The funny thing is that Hausmann et al. had to conclude that these growth accelerations are unpredictable; that the vast majority of them are unrelated to standard growth recipes.

Easterly notes that South Korea, for example, started to demonstrate spectacular growth rates, after the aid had declined[46]. The flipside of this same coin is what happened in Sub-Saharan Africa during the past three decades: whilst aid increased steeply, growth of the typical African recipient country deteriorated sharply[47]. I am sure Easterly did not want to suggest that aid at large has not been useful. After all, aid greatly contributed to improvement in health: smallpox has been eradicated, infant mortality rates have been lowered, and illnesses such as diarrhea and river blindness have been combated quite effectively. Aid has improved women and girls' access to education and modern contraception. Without foreign financial support the fight against aids would be bleaker, especially in Africa. The *Green Revolution* was also made possible by foreign aid. Millions and millions of victims of natural disasters have been helped by donor governments and by the generosity of private citizens. Peace has been restored, financed by donors, in countries such as Sierra Leone, Liberia, Kosovo and East Timor. Moreover, what some aid critics tend to forget is that aid has often prevented poor countries from sinking deeper in misery, thereby ensuring some political and social stability.

Yet, it has proved difficult to sustain economic growth with aid. Sometimes I compare this dilemma with a poorly performing Second Division football club facing the challenge to reach Champions League levels. This seems a near impossible task, which surely cannot be achieved overnight. Especially not when the club does not have the financial resources to buy good players (the good ones having left) or afford a successful trainer/coach. Worse, the club's managers have not thought of a medium term strategy to improve performance. Most players are not "team players" because they do not trust each other. And to complete the dismal picture, some of them make secret deals "selling" games. Altogether, the challenge seems near impossible.

Development requires patience. And this is precisely what development ministers of donor countries do not have. Their "expiry date" is roughly four years. Hence, they want to show results quickly to satisfy their constituencies and parliaments. They have little to show for in the realm of growth. But economic growth is crucial to making aid redundant, curbing corruption, violence and terrorism, limiting human misery, creating an environment in which women, men and children can use their talents and contribute to economic development. And it is also economic growth that helps to improve the quality of institutions[48].

There is no specific Millennium Development Goal (MDG) directed at the promotion of economic growth. This is all the more surprising because although in many poor countries health and education coverage has improved, this achievement has not been transformed into better incomes and employment for the poor. The tension between bringing about growth on the one hand and the need to show quick results on the other probably best explains the endless succession of growth panaceas, none of which worked as far as sustained economic growth of the poorest countries is concerned. An additional problem is that new panaceas do not replace old ones; they just add to the already very broad development agendas of the donors.

Aid agencies have followed the Dirigiste Dogma for too long; in other words, state-led development. The past 20 years has seen the death of centrally planned economies, stagnation in the leading import-substituting models and colossal economic failure of post-independent Africa, which pursued a state-led development strategy.

It took the donor community quite some time before they started to appreciate the crucial role of private sector development, which holds the key to economic growth. The 2005 World Development Report *A Better Investment Climate for Everyone* is just one proof of this recent attention. *Economic Growth in the 1990s* as well as Rodrik et al. emphasize the promotion of economic growth as the central challenge that developing countries face. This is a constructive step in the right direction. However, taking away the most binding constraints which hinder economic growth is one thing, sustaining it is another. Hausmann, Rodrik, and Velasco's model suggests that once the principal binding constraint has been identified, the next steps involve tackling the reasons for that constraint, so as to arrive in the course of time at a situation of sustained economic growth. These reasons include, amongst many others, institutional and governance aspects, such as the poor adherence to property rights and corruption. Resolving them implies political decisions, which may prove difficult to achieve in poor countries characterized by political and institutional frameworks intent to maintain the status quo.

Conclusions

In the final analysis it is developing countries themselves who define their economic destiny. Aid may help finance some factors that promise growth, but in adverse conditions, it may not. Some developing countries fared well over the past fifty years while most did not. Economic growth and the question of how to accelerate – and sustain – it over time implies more than capital and labor accumulation. It also implies productivity growth: policies, institutions and, deep down, the role of societies' aptitudes and attitudes towards growth. Unfortunately, some societies are more congenial to economic achievement and advance than others, and the poor countries of this world so far have not demonstrated great talents in economic achievement, thereby refuting the equity postulate which many development economists implicitly take for granted.

Yet, aid definitely helped improve health conditions, access to and quality of water and sanitation, as well as access to education. It promoted necessary leaps forward, such as the Green Revolution. Aid helped restore peace and it prevented many countries from sinking deeper into misery.

The big challenge for aid agencies is finding out how to adjust their policies so that their financial and technical assistance contribute more effectively to sustained economic growth of poor countries. General recommendations to improve aid-delivery gain relevance if translated to specific recipient country contexts, as alluded to by *Economic Growth in the 1990s* and Rodrik's proposals on the matter. These specific country contexts should form the basis of any aid intervention. Moreover, the interventions should primarily be geared to the promotion of economic growth, since growth – in turn – promotes institutional and other improvements in areas such as those health and education. Hence, aid interventions should *not* take as their point of departure donor agencies' development policies often resulting in a "spray gun" approach taken by them. Many donors believe that running projects, for instance, in education, environmental protection, gender and human rights, as well as infrastructure and police reform, all at the same time, is *the* way forward. It is not. It shows a lack of strategic insight into the dynamic forces that lie behind growth processes of recipient countries.

Apart from adjusting their aid policies, donors should also adjust their staff composition, hiring experts in private sector development – people who know how the private sector and banks and the like function, how markets function, how commercial risks can be calculated, and so forth. Furthermore, aid ministers and presidents of development banks will have to make sure that mainstream thinking within their institutions is directed to the promotion of private sector development, perhaps at the detriment of powerful social sector departments.

State-led growth has not worked. A healthy mix of private sector development supported by stimulating government policies, as applied by the Asian Tigers for instance, would be a better bet. However, with the demise of the Washington Consensus, and the emergence of orthodox socialist governments, especially in Latin America, state-led growth is re-emerging. This, to my mind, is an unfortunate development, not only because overwhelming evidence shows that it has not worked in developing countries' contexts, but also because their public sectors are by and large inefficient and absolutely not equipped to lead economic growth. Sure enough, the State has an important role to play in creating a favorable business environment, and to correct market failures. Yet, the State has in many instances proved *not* to be an appropriate promoter of growth.

Aid does not necessarily have to be spent within recipient countries. The literature and practice tell us that the poorest developing countries, in particular, have limited aid absorption capacities leading to waste and diminishing returns. Examples of aid spent for the benefit of these poor countries, but outside them, would be investing in research that would benefit them, or to guarantee the purchase of medicines developed by the pharmaceutical industry. Another useful investment would be to help developing countries in their preparation for international trade negotiations, such as the Doha Round. Aid can be used more efficiently and effectively. This, in turn, may help improve the aid absorption capacity of recipient countries and even turn diminishing returns of aid into increasing returns.

Since the 1990s, aid has been directed more and more to help developing countries with good policies and institutions, leaving behind those without them. As a belated reaction there is now increasing attention on how to help failed states, as well as to help fragile and failing states, which could slide down to that dismal level. The question is what can – and should – the international donor community do to prevent this from happening, and what could be done to help get these states back on the road to stability and economic growth.

The promotion of economic growth regained prominence in the development debate. This is more than justified, as economic growth is the only impulse that can help overcome misery, political instability, and poverty. Boosting economic growth is not as difficult as sustaining it over time. The latter implies taking political decisions that may be hard to achieve. Donors share a responsibility to help promote and sustain economic growth in aid dependent countries. They will have to adjust their aid policies, targeting them to help overcome binding constraints to growth. These constraints may not only be tackled in the recipient country, but may also include unfair trade relations, which donor countries must correct. Aid is important, but in the final analysis it is most important that people in poor countries do avail themselves of stable employment and income.

A final point. Will theoreticians be able to provide us with the universal economic growth model? Although some scholars say they cannot, I have not given up hope for two reasons. First, there are, without any doubt, universal characteristics of growth processes, irrespective of cultural, political and institutional settings. Second, men are curious and want to understand how things work. And it is unresolved questions, such as what might the factors of economic growth be, that inspire the best minds to look for answers.

References

Bauer, P., 1976: *Dissent on Development* (Cambridge MA: Harvard University Press)

Bauer, P., 2000: *From Subsistence to Exchange* (Princeton: Princeton University Press)

Birdsall, N., Rodrik, D., Subramanian, A., 2005: *How to Help Poor Countries* (Foreign Affairs, July/August)

Boone, P., 1996: *Politics, and the Effectiveness of Foreign Aid* (European Economic Review, 40 (2))

Burnside, C., Dollar, D., 2000: *Aid, Policies and Growth* (American Economic Review, September, 90:4)

Burnside, C., Dollar, D., 2004: *Aid, Policies, And Growth: Revisiting the Evidence* (Washington DC: World Bank Policy Research Working Paper 3251, March)

Clemens, M., Radelet, S., Bhavnani, R., 2004: *Counting Chickens when They Hatch: The Short-Term Effect of Aid on Growth* (Center for Global Development: Working Paper, no. 44, November)

Collier, P., Dehn, J., 2001: *Aid, Shocks, and Growth* (Washington DC: World Bank Policy Research Paper 2688, October)

Easterly, W., 2002: *The Elusive Quest for Growth: Economists' Adventures and Misadventures in the Tropics* (Cambridge MA: The MIT Press)

Easterly, W., 2003: *Can Foreign Aid Buy Growth?* (Journal of Economic Perspectives, Vol. 17, no. 3)

Easterly, W., 2003: *The Cartel of Good Intentions: The Problem of Bureaucracy in Foreign Aid* (Policy Reform, Vol. 00)

Easterly, W., Levine, R., Roodman, D., 2003: *New Data, New Doubts: A Comment on Burnside and Dollar's "Aid, Policies, and Growth"* (Cambridge, MA: National Bureau of Economic Research, July)

Glaeser, E., La Porta, R., Lopez-de-Salinas, F., Shleifer, A., 2004: *Do Institutions Cause Growth?* (Cambridge, MA: National Bureau of Economic Research Working Paper Series)

Griffin, K., 1970: *Foreign Capital, Domestic Savings and Economic Development* (Bulletin of the Oxford University Institute of Economics and Statistics, 32 (2))

Hansen, H., Tarp, F., 2001: *Aid and Growth Regressions* (Journal of Development Economics, Vol. 64)

Hausmann, R., Pritchett, L., Rodrik, D., 2004: *Growth Accelerations* (Cambridge MA: National Bureau of Economic Research Working Paper 10566, June)

Hausmann, R., Rodrik, D., Velasco, A., 2004: *Growth Diagnostics* (Cambridge MA: John F. Kennedy School of Management, Harvard University, first version September)

Kenny, C., Williams, D., 2000: *What Do We Know About Economic Growth? Or, Why Don't We Know Very Much* (World Development, Vol. 29, no.1)

Lal, D., 2000: *The Poverty of Development Economics* (Cambridge MA: The MIT Press)

North, D., 1990: *Institutions, Institutional Change and Economic Performance* (Cambridge: Cambridge University Press)

OECD, 2003: *Final ODA Data for 2003* (Paris. OECD)

Papanek, G., 1972: *The Effects of Aid and Other Resource Transfers on Savings and Growth in Less Developed Countries* (Economic Journal, 82 (327))

Rajan, R., Subramanian, A., 2005: *Aid and Growth: Revisiting the Evidence* (Washington DC: IMF Working Paper,June)

Rajan, R., Subramanian, A., 2005: *What Undermines Aid's Impact on Growth?* (Washington DC: IMF Working Paper, June)

Rodrik, D., 2004: *Growth Strategies* (Cambridge MA: John F. Kennedy School of Management, Harvard University, August)

Rodrik, D., 2004: *Rethinking Growth Policies in the Developing World* (Cambridge MA: Harvard University, Draft of the Luca d'Agliano Lecture, October)

Rodrik, D., 2006: *Goodbye Washington Consensus, Hello Washington Confusion?* (Cambridge MA: Harvard University, January)

Roodman, D., 2004: *The Anarchy of Numbers: Aid, Development, and Cross-Country Empirics* (Center for Global Development, Working Paper, no. 32, July)

Rostow, W., 1971: *The Stages of Economic Growth* (Cambridge: Cambridge University Press)

UNCTAD, 2004: *World Investment Report 2004*

World Bank, 1998: *Assessing Aid; What Works, What Doesn't, and Why* (New York: Oxford University Press)

World Bank, 2005: *World Development Report 2005; A Better Investment Climate for Everyone* (New York: Oxford University Press)

World Bank, 2005: *Economic Growth in the 1990s, Learning from a Decade of Reform* (Washington DC: World Bank)

Globalization, Growth, and Poverty

Introduction

George Bernard Shaw is not only remembered for his plays and – together with fellow Irishman, Oscar Wilde – for his bons mots, he also wrote two volumes entitled: *The Intelligent Woman's Guide to Socialism, Capitalism, Sovietism and Fascism*. Therein he explained the differences between these ideologies, inspired by questions asked by Mary Stewart Cholmondeley, his sister-in-law.

Ideologies and religions inspired throughout the ages heated debates, and from time to time led to war. I believe they did – and still do – because they touch upon the deepest convictions and emotions of human beings. Should Shaw have lived today, he could have written about neo-liberalism, globalization, and the World Trade Organization (WTO). All these topics function in the eyes of their opponents like a red cape in front of a bull. These opponents, often hailing from erstwhile communist and socialist backgrounds, are so well organized that they effectively frustrated a string of WTO summits as well as World Bank and IMF annual meetings. They attack neo-liberalism and globalization with arguments that at first glance sell well in the media. However, confronted with the facts, most – not all – turn out to be counterproductive to the opponents' very objectives: creating fair opportunities for poor countries, eradicating poverty and creating a more equitable global society.

The intriguing question about these opponents is why are they so blind to empirical evidence? They radiate a deep hatred to the very economic phenomena that may help develop poor countries; instead they consider them exploitative and unjust. What is it that inspires this narrow-minded and intolerant attitude? The other day I came across an article by the famous Turkish writer Orhan Pamuk who gave a troubling answer to this question. His article deals with the tensions between poor and rich countries. Pamuk says about a typical inhabitant of a poor country that: "...*he senses in a corner of his mind that his poverty is to some considerable degree the fault of his own folly and inadequacy, or those of his father and grandfather. The western world is scarcely aware of this overwhelming feeling of humiliation that is experienced by most of the world's population*"[49]. Pamuk puts a large part of the blame on failing economic policies of the leadership of poor countries. I will try to provide a balanced picture of the debate and the results of globalization, thereby dealing with the most important popular observations about this phenomenon.

Globalization; what is meant by it

Let us first establish what is meant by globalization. Stanley Hoffmann, amongst others, identifies three types of globalization: economic, cultural and political[50]. This essay only deals with the first type: economic globalization. Economic globalization is defined in various forms. Martin Wolf, for example, describes the term in his excellent book *Why Globalization Works*, as follows: "Globalization is no fanatical ideology, but a name for the process of integration across frontiers of liberalizing market economies, at a time of rapidly falling costs of transport and communications"[51]. Jagdish Bhagwati's more accurate definition runs as follows: "Economic globalization constitutes integration of national economies into the international economy through trade, direct foreign investment (by corporations and multinationals), short-term capital flows, international flows of workers and humanity generally, and flows of technology"[52]. Thomas Friedman compares globalization with a system like the Cold War system: "Globalization has its own rules and logic that today directly or indirectly influence the politics, environments, geopolitics and economics of virtually every country in the world"[53].

The description of globalization I like best is the one provided by Timothy Taylor in The Public Interest which was quoted in an article in the Herald Tribune. It runs as follows: *"Globalization is not a magic cure-all for what ails a nation's economy, nor is it a plot by profit-hungry mega-corporations to exploit workers and spoil the environment. Globalization is not the return of colonialism, nor is it the arrival of world government. At the most fundamental level globalization simply means an expansion of the range of possible commercial activities. Seeking out and sorting through the possibilities opened up by globalization will require a daunting amount of effort, flexibility, and change, precisely because globalization embodies such a vast and marvelous array of new economic opportunities"*.

This essay intends to demonstrate that those who take up the challenge of globalization can indeed benefit from the marvelous array of new economic opportunities, and thus see their growth figures go up, a result that, in turn, greatly helps to diminish poverty.

Those in favor and those against

Though the opponents of globalization seem to have the upper hand in the debate and in public opinion, the facts point to a different direction. The World Economic Forum commissioned an opinion poll in preparation of its February 2002 meeting in New York. It surveyed an urban sample of 1000 individuals in each of 25 countries, and virtually everywhere a majority viewed globalization favorably. But, there was also evidence of an ironic reversal: the developing counties showed greater majorities in favor of globalization, whereas earlier, the opposite would have been true. Thus, while there was much skepticism about globalization in the developing countries in the nearly three decades following the end of the Second World War, and an opposite pro-globalization attitude in the developed countries, this has now been turned upside down[54].

Yet the opponents, who form a minority, represent a rather formidable counterforce. This force will gain more ground if a worldwide recession would occur, for instance, triggered by a collapse of

China's financial system or by a monetary crisis, inspired by the growing US current account deficit. Labor unions in countries that stand to loose employment opportunities could exert irresistible pressure; protectionism and nationalism could reappear, and inequality as well as poverty worldwide will not diminish further. In other words, the process of globalization is not necessarily here to stay, it may very well be interrupted by the counterforces I just mentioned.

The waves of globalization and their effects

Globalization is not a new phenomenon. A first wave of globalization ruled the world roughly around the turn of the nineteenth century. Ironically enough, Marx and Engels predicted it in their Communist Manifesto[55]. This first wave was brought to an abrupt halt when the Great War began. It reappeared after the Second World War, subsided a bit in the 1970s, but came back in full force after 1980. What did these waves mean for growth, equality and poverty reduction? Each of them had their specific characteristics, however, the driving forces for all the waves were technological advance – mainly in transport and communications – combined with favorable world trade policies.

The first wave

The first wave, spanning the period 1870-1914, triggered a massive increase in the flows of goods, capital and labor[56]. Exports relative to world income nearly doubled to about 8%. Foreign capital more than trebled relative to income in the colonies and developing countries of Africa, Asia and Latin America. And what may surprise us now is that migration boomed even more. Sixty million people migrated from impoverished parts of Europe to North America, as so dramatically depicted by the immigration office (turned museum) at New York's Ellis Island. What is less well-known is that South-South labor flows were also impressive: the flows from very poor and densely populated China and India to less densely populated Sri Lanka, Burma, Thailand, the Philippines and Vietnam were probably of the same magnitude as the movements of poor Europeans to the New World. All told, 10% of the world's population migrated to greener pastures at the time.

What did all these changes mean for progress and poverty? Global income per capita rose at an unprecedented rate, but not fast enough to prevent the numbers of poor people from rising. Among the globalizing countries there was convergence in income per capita, primarily driven by migration. The bad news was that the gap between the globalizers and those countries left behind was widening; world inequality widened. The boom in international trade, investment, and migration collapsed at the beginning of the First World War.

The second wave

The period after the Second World War – roughly spanning 1950 to 1970 – can be identified with the second wave; also known as the *Golden Age* of economic development. The terrible consequences of the previous retreat into nationalism gave rise to internationalism immediately after the Second World War. This was also the time when Alfred Sauvy introduced the term Third World. That was not surprising as the second wave promoted economic integration of Europe, North America, and Japan, whereas most developing countries remained stuck in primary commodity exporting and were largely isolated from international capital flows.

The countries belonging to the Organization of Economic Cooperation and Development (OECD) economically converged thanks to unprecedented growth rates. Within them was a modest trend towards greater equality, promoted by redistribution and social welfare programs. It should be noted that growth in the developing countries also recovered, but less strongly. Hence, the gap between rich and poor countries continued to increase. There was little net change in the distribution of income among and within developing countries. At the beginning of the second wave development assistance was introduced, often in the form of a continuation of former colonial relationships. Development assistance had strong ideological connotations. It was seen by some as an antidote to the unjust, exploitative functioning of the world economy. Aid was used by the superpowers as an instrument to gain Third World support in the fight against communism or capitalism.

The third wave

This started around 1980 and is continuing today. It was spurred by a lowering of tariffs, technological advance in transport and communication technologies, as well as by the choice of large developing countries, notably China and India, to improve their investment climates and to open up to foreign trade and investment. For the first time, poor countries were able to harness the potential of their abundant labor to break into global markets for manufactured goods and for services. Manufactures, for example, rose from less than a quarter of developing country exports in 1980 to more than 80 percent by 1998. Some 24 developing countries – where 3 billion people live – have doubled their ratio of trade to income over the past twenty years[57].

However, the rest of the developing world trades less today than it did twenty years ago. The more globalized developing countries have increased their per capita growth rate from 1 percent in the 1960s to 3 percent in the 1970s, 4 percent in the 1980s, and 5 percent in the 1990s[58]. Their growth rates eclipse those of the OECD countries. Hence, the new globalizers are *catching up*. The dark side of these results is that much of the rest of the developing world – where 2 billion people live – is falling behind. Their aggregate growth rate was actually negative in the 1990s. These countries are in decline and poverty is increasing.

As for migration, this is not so dramatic as the migration triggered by the first wave. About 120 million people (2 percent of the world's population) live in foreign countries nowadays. Roughly half of them live in rich countries and the other half in poor countries. However, because the population of developing countries is about five times greater than the population of the developed ones, migrants comprise a larger share (6 percent) of the population in rich countries than in poor ones (1 percent). In other words, the third wave is not being accompanied by massive migration, as we saw in the first wave of globalization. This is no doubt inspired by the fact that many high-income countries deliberately limit the inflow of migrants, mainly for political reasons. For example, in quite a few European countries the erstwhile influx of immigrants has led to tensions and, sometimes, riots. Ultra-conservative political parties have sprung up in countries such as Belgium, Germany, the Netherlands and Switzerland, who use immigrants (often from Muslim countries) as scapegoats for economic and social short-comings in their societies. These political *reflexes* do not make sense in economic terms. Migration is the oldest reaction against poverty. It is good for the country to which they go and it helps to break the equilibrium of poverty in the country from which migrants came. Moreover, demographic projections (i.e., more old and less young people) indicate that Europe, for example, will need a continued influx of migrants if it wants to keep on growing. Thanks to immigration, its workforce will remain large enough to help finance a reasonable level of social security, including pensions for its older population. The implication of this demographic trend will in future be valid for many other countries, including China.

What effect does the present wave of globalization have on inequality? Within the globalizing developing countries, inequality has only seen small changes. In some countries, such as in the Philippines and Malaysia, inequality declined. Vietnam, for example, managed to register a large growth in per capita income accompanied by significant changes in inequality. It also managed to reduce the level of absolute poverty by half over the course of the past ten years.

But in Latin America, wage inequality widened as a result of prior extreme inequalities, as well as a result of adverse governance environments. In China too inequality has risen but this is less problematic. Initially, China was both extremely equal and extremely poor. Since the mid 1980s there has been rapid growth in urban agglomerations, which has increased inequality, as the gap between rural and urban areas has widened. But, if this increase in inequality has been the price for growth, it has paid off in terms of a massive reduction in poverty. The number of rural poor declined from 250 million in 1978 to just 34 million in 1999, according to the World Bank[59]. In a Survey of The Economist, World Bank's representative in China, David Dollar, even says: "We have a lot of confidence that poverty has been almost eradicated"[60].

As already mentioned, 2 billion people, populations of those countries in Sub-Saharan Africa and the former Soviet Union "who missed the boat", do not yet benefit from globalization[61]. What is their influence on world inequality? On balance, statistics indicate that since 1980 world inequality has stopped increasing, and may have started to fall. Although participation in the world's industrial economy raises incomes, for about a century only a minority of people (i.e., inhabitants of the now rich countries) participated in this economy and so global industrialization led to greater inequality. The present third wave, however, may mark the turning point at which participation has widened sufficiently for it to reduce both poverty and inequality[62].

Possible trend

If global trade liberalization were to continue in the future, it would offer enormous opportunities for developing countries to expand their trade and increase welfare. The World Bank suggests that world income in 2015 would be USD 355 billion a year *higher* with merchandise-trade liberalization (in 1997 dollars). The developing countries would gain USD 184 billion annually, of which USD 121 billion would be the benefits derived from their own liberalization, whilst the rest would come from liberalization by high-income countries. Nearly 80 percent of the gains to developing countries would come from liberalization of agriculture. With dynamic benefits added, the Bank estimates that developing countries' incomes would rise by more than USD 500 billion a year, with

USD 390 billion of this coming from agriculture and USD 120 billion from textiles and clothing. To put this in context, the total GDP of developing countries at market prices was USD 3,600 billion in 2000[63].

Is globalization a threat as the opponents say?

Radical left-leaning economic philosophers, some trade unions in high-wage countries, quite a few Non-Governmental Organizations (NGOs) and politicians of the extreme left, vehemently oppose globalization, and flatly reject what Timothy Taylor said about "the marvelous array of new economic opportunities". Indeed, globalization in their eyes would appear to be a plot of profit-hungry mega-corporations to exploit workers and spoil the environment.

What these critics forget is that it *takes two to tango*, i.e., the failure to benefit from globalization is not so much globalization's fault. No, it must also be explained in terms of the inadequate responses of developing countries to offer an appropriate business environment to harness the opportunities and benefits provided by globalization.

What is the critique comprised of? Let us follow Martin Wolf's excellent summary and take eight of the nine points of the critique he deals with[64]. Here they are:

1. Imports from low-wage developing countries hollow out the industries of high-income countries and make it impossible for high-wage, rich countries to compete without a collapse in their wage levels.
2. The competitive advantage of developing countries is based on exploitation of their workers, including children.
3. Global free trade is destructive for the environment.
4. Liberal global trade should be replaced by localization.
5. Free trade undermines the development strategies of developing countries, which cannot compete with the advanced technologies of the high-income countries.

6. Trade in commodities is unfair and unrewarding for developing countries.
7. The World Trade Organization (WTO) is an anti-democratic organization, run in the interests of transnational corporations and is threatening to national autonomy, the environment and human welfare.
8. High-income countries are hypocritical in their imposition of free trade upon developing countries, since they remain protectionist themselves, particularly in areas of most interest to developing countries.

The critique comes from different types of opponents. As demonstrated below, most of it does not make sense, but some does. Let us deal with the critique point by point.

Imports from low-wage developing countries hollow out the industries of high-income countries

This sounds logical. How can rich country workers compete with their far cheaper Chinese counterparts? Let us look at the facts. It is true that the average Chinese worker is many times cheaper than the average German or American worker, however, what really counts is their respective productivity. The average Chinese worker produces USD 2,900 of value added annually, whereas an American adds USD 81,000 value annually, and a German worker USD 80,000[65]. What explains this huge divide in productivity? First, the American and European worker avails himself of much more capital at his command than a Chinese one. Second, across the board they are far better educated than the Chinese. The Chinese worker still lacks experience with sophisticated management and manufacturing practices. And, finally, China produces labor-intensive products, such as garments, whose value added is much lower than the technologically sophisticated American or European products. There is no doubt that the Chinese will catch up in productivity terms. What then? This will mean that their real wage rate will go up accordingly, as the development of South Korea has demonstrated, for example. Today, South Korea's wages are on average fifty times higher than China's.

Another question is why has employment in manufacturing in high-income countries fallen over the past few decades? Is this because of competition from emerging developing country economies or are the reasons to be found in internal economic dynamics? Martin Wolf provides the following explanation: labor productivity rose in high-income countries across the board faster than the business sector as a whole, which implied that employment in manufacturing had to shrink relative to the business sector as a whole, if output merely rose at the same rate in the two sectors. But people in high-income countries also tend to spend a declining share of their incomes on manufactures and an increasing share on services. The combination of halting growth in demand for manufactures with rapid rises in productivity guarantees a steep fall in the share of employment in manufacturing in the years ahead, regardless of what happens to trade balances[66]. The downward employment trend we see in manufacturing in high-income countries was preceded by the steeply downward trend in employment in agriculture in the same countries.

But this is not the complete picture. Now, suppose that China exports products in line with its comparative advantage to Europe or the United States, then the terms of trade – and thus real incomes – will improve for the latter. This means that importing countries can buy more with what it produces. And that is why China's entry into the world markets is beneficial for the high-income countries that produce the computers, airplanes, medical equipment and other sophisticated goods that the Chinese wish to buy. Trade, in other words, provides the best of both worlds.

Unfair competition thanks to exploitation of workers and child labor

This is a highly compelling argument. Pictures of slaving female workers in hot and unventilated production halls, eight year olds knotting carpets or sewing footballs; who has not seen these pictures, and who does not instantly feel appalled? But let us look a bit deeper and put the argument in its proper context.

First, we should appreciate *why* people are prepared to work under such circumstances. The simple answer is this: to step out of their poverty trap. The incomes these poor workers earn, and the prospect of future employment, makes an enormous difference. They can think of sending their children to school, buying better health services and so forth. In other words, there is hope for a better future. But, what about the protection of workers' rights? Suppose that strong labor unions would be successful in raising wages and conditions for their members. The price of labor would superficially rise and the labor market would then become dualistic: one part protected with inflated wages blocking further industrialization, while the other part continues to provide low wages for the vast majority of the workers. This is what happened in India, where the labor market controlled by unions only absorbs 5 million workers. Compare this to what happened in South Korea, for instance, where the unions initially were not able to divide the labor market. In South Korea the workers earn nowadays much more than their Indian counterparts. That is the result of rapid growth of output *and* employment in a profitable modern sector to a tighter overall labor market. This is the path China is following at the moment.

As for child labor, around 250 million children between the ages of five and fourteen work in developing countries, although this number is lower now than at any time in history. Of these, seventy percent work in agriculture and 10-15 million in export industries, especially in the Asian sub-continent. These children work, not because their parents are worse than parents in high-income countries, but for the simple reason that the parents are too poor to send their children to school. But the future is bright because birth rates in developing countries are declining, which means that parents are relying less and less on their children for their survival and old age. Moreover, rising wages have a positive influence on schooling and health, and a diminishing influence on child labor. In Vietnam, for example, the income of the poorest 10 percent of the population rose by more than half over the past decade and this led to a sharp reduction in child labor and a greater investment in their education. Campaigns in the West to stop child labor may have very adverse effects if they are not accompanied by measures to provide proper financial compensation for the parents, as well as a decent education for their children. Banning exports of products made by children will probably have negative effects on the children (and their parents) concerned. They may fall prey to worse paid and more dangerous jobs, or end up in child prostitution or the like.

The environment is the victim of globalization

Globalization implies economic growth, intensive transportation and energy to produce goods. Well-known expressions to lament globalization's inevitable assault on the environment is: *the race to the bottom* and the creation of *pollution havens*. However, evidence has shown that economic growth correlates positively with care for the environment[67]. Note that market economies have been far less environmentally damaging than economies based on central planning, including China's (China is the second largest emitter of CO_2, after the US). Some scholars maintain that there is such a thing as an environmental *Kuznets curve*. In some aspects there is, such as the quality of air and water. In general, however, there is not.

During the present wave of globalization, the new globalizers have indeed increased their share of global industrial production. This has increased their share of pollution-intensive industries. However, this increase was *not* related to exporting as it largely met domestic demand. Developing countries harnessed their comparative advantage in labor-intensive industries, not in pollution-intensive industries. They have also not increased their share of global pollution-intensive industrial exports. Pollution-intensive industries of the new globalizers are mainly meeting local demand, justifying the question of whether environmental degradation is to be attributed to globalization. As it happens, its influence is exaggerated. More energy, for instance, is used in local rather than in international trade. Deforestation is frequently not caused by exports but by land-hunger and poverty. Pressure on dry land, such as in the Sahel countries, is a result of overpopulation (of man and animals) and of ineffective enforcement of property rights.

Limiting the environmental damage of economic growth and globalization is a matter of political will. This has been overwhelmingly demonstrated in the vast majority of high-income countries, where public opinion combined with appropriate legislation helped to dramatically improve environmental conditions. Environmental regulations in developing countries are being tightened, but, for various reasons, many are simply not yet implementing pollution abatement measures that are readily available, cheap and effective.

Environmental threats such as global warming, caused by the industrial countries' use of fossil fuels that turn into greenhouse gases (CO_2), the hole in the ozone layer caused by the use of chlorofluorocarbons (CFCs) and the pollution of oceans, require worldwide commitment and action. And that is far less easy to achieve. Observers note that the Kyoto protocol is deficient, not even taking into consideration that the United States does not form part of it. At the end of the day the obstacle to preserving the environment is the unwillingness of countries to impose a high cost upon processes and activities that generate greenhouse gases, CFCs and the like.

Localization

This is probably the most ludicrous proposal by the opponents of globalization. What do they mean by "localization"? Under localization the economy would be under full collective control, but at a local level. Each country would have an obligation to balance its trade. It would also discriminate in favor of local production, insisting that companies would need to locate in the country (or region) if they wished to sell their products there. The objective of this proposal is to end ruthless competition generated by globalization. In other words: back to the world of Jean Jacques Rousseau! The aim is self-sufficiency, in which each locality, region or nation only imports what it cannot reasonably produce for itself. The half-wits who promote this idea call themselves *new millennium collectivists*. From the report of the International Forum on Globalization I quote the following: "If people grow their own food, produce their own necessities and control the conditions of their lives, the issue of price becomes irrelevant"[68]. Now back to real life. Subsistence farming is a risky strategy. Just be reminded of the millions of North Koreans who are starving, thanks to the trade policies implemented by their rulers. Food accounted in the 1990s for more than 20 percent of imports in twenty least-developed countries and for 40 percent in four of them. Being able to buy food anywhere in the world is a far more secure position for a country to be in.

Efficiency would not be promoted any longer for lack of competition and the need to innovate. There would not be intra-industry trade, nor trade in parts and components that helped boost productivity in most countries. The new millennium collectivists maintain that in the long run prices do not matter. This in fact implies that the inefficient use of resources also does not matter, as one of the big efforts made by competitive companies is to reduce the use of resources. This is why there have been such large increases in output per unit of energy over the past three decades, amongst others, thanks to the steep increase in the price of oil. This effort would also disappear if these collectivists had their way.

How can Sub-Saharan African countries ever develop if they were to be condemned to self-sufficiency? They would be forced to continue exporting raw materials such as cocoa, coffee, tea, cotton and some minerals, whose prices are not only volatile but also show a structurally decreasing tendency in comparison to the prices of manufactures. These poor African countries would be unable to make a single manufactured product that high-income countries cannot make. Developing countries will be condemned to continue exporting the products mentioned above, most would have no capacity to import any of the high-technology products. If the policy of localization would be pushed to its logical conclusion, developing countries would cease to trade among themselves too, since few would be able to make anything others cannot, and hence, will be left to consume what they produce, and nothing else.

In the 1960s the small island of Mauritius, off Africa's South East Coast, was supposed to have no future. It did not have any natural resources apart from sugar. It had a small and impoverished population (700,000) and the nearby (African) markets were far away and did not have purchasing power. However, it achieved a 4.7 percent annual increase in real GDP per head between 1975 and 2001, amongst others, thanks to the establishment of an Export Processing Zone. Mauritius prospered by taking advantage of opportunities for export of labor-intensive products, initially clothing. Today, Mauritius has a population of around 1 million with a GDP per head of around USD 10,000 at Purchasing Power Parity (PPP). Should Mauritius have followed localization it would have been as poor today as it was during the 1960s.

Let me provide some more figures. In 2000, developing countries exported USD 1,060 billion worth of manufactures, which accounted for 71 percent of their total merchandise exports. They imported USD 1,616 billion worth of merchandise of all kinds. If their merchandise exports were eliminated, as the new millennium collectivists recommend, their merchandise imports would need to fall by two-thirds. This represents a reduction in trade that would result from full localization, since temperate agricultural commodities and even minerals can be supplied within the countries to which they now export, provided they are sufficiently indifferent to the costs of doing so.

Economic self-sufficiency is perhaps only possible in a country like the United States, and even the US is dependent on oil imports for their energy needs and on cheap labor to do the jobs that Americans are no longer prepared to do. All other countries depend for their development and welfare on importing and exporting goods and services. Where economic self-sufficiency has been tried, such as in North Korea and Cuba, it failed miserably to generate prosperity. That the new millennium collectivists promote themselves as the friends of the poor demonstrates how shortsighted they really are. With friends like these, the poor of the world need no enemies!

Free trade undermines the development of poor countries

The promoters of this point of view are much more sophisticated and balanced than the "localizers" who want to go back to the days of Rousseau. They recognize that working market institutions are a necessary condition for long-term success. But they resist the idea that across-the-board trade liberalization would be a sufficient, or even necessary condition for rapid economic development. Nobody would deny this. Trade liberalization on its own – regardless of the circumstances – will not generate rapid growth.

The views of two critics will be dealt with next. The first one is Ha-Joon Chang, a South Korean scholar whose ideas are included in *Kicking Away the Ladder*[69]. The other is Dani Rodrik, who has written various books and articles on globalization. Chang argues that active industrial trade and technology policies are necessary for socializing the risks involved in the development of infant industries. He makes this argument on the basis of an interesting historical analysis of the successful economies of today, starting with the first industrializer, the United Kingdom. All of them, notably the US, Germany, France, Sweden, Belgium and, later on, Japan, South Korea and Taiwan, used a range of active protectionist measures to overcome backwardness and promote industrial development. The exception to Chang's reasoning was, amongst others, the Netherlands which applied laissez faire. Being overwhelmingly a commercial country, the Netherlands never really established a firm industrial base. Recent exceptions to Chang's thinking are Singapore and Hong Kong.

Chang admits that the promotion of industrial development through protection is not the only road to development. He admits that the fact that the use of activist industrial, trade and technology policies is necessary does not imply that all countries that use such policies are guaranteed economic success. What it does mean, says Chang, is that developing countries *must be granted the opportunity* to apply such policies, otherwise they are kicking away the ladder up which they themselves climb.

Dani Rodrik's central argument is that the benefits of trade liberalization have been greatly exaggerated. Policymakers should focus on the *fundamentals* of economic growth: investment, macro-economic stability, human resources and good governance, and not let international economic integration dominate their thinking[70]. Rodrik agrees that successful economies become more open, but he also says, making an economy more open – by lowering tariff barriers – does not guarantee success. On the contrary, Rodrik points to the import substitution strategies that, he says, were successful before 1973. They failed since then, says Rodrik, because they could not sustain macro-economic stability.

This is an argument in favor of import substitution not often heard, as it is widely accepted in the economic literature that import substitution did much more harm than good, especially in Latin America, where it was widely applied. Martin Wolf's response to Rodrik's argument is that particularly in the absence of offsetting incentives to export, infant industry protection is highly inefficient. The emerging Asian economies all took the export-led growth model that worked, whereas import substitution failed to promote sustained economic growth.

Jeffrey Sachs explains in more detail why import substitution did not work in Latin America[71]. Latin America simply did not have the necessary technology or the R&D capacity to build up industries that would have been able to compete with those on the other side of their tariff barriers. Furthermore, the internal markets were relatively small (export markets are for developing country exporters infinitely larger), and there was little interest in regional integration at the time. The industries thus created evolved into oligopolistic or monopolistic entities with little drive – due to a lack of competition – for productivity improvement. The intimate relationship between many Latin American governments and industry often resulted in perverse decisions, in that not always the most effective investments were chosen to promote a country's development; personal interests often had the upper hand.

In conclusion, one has to accept that much more is involved in successful development than trade policy alone. It is also true that quite a few successful countries applied protectionist policies before entering the world market. The creation of indigenous technological capacities has demanded special efforts of developing countries, and it *did* pay off. That is what most opponents of globalization often forget: that globalization cannot be blamed for failing policies of those developing countries that do not seize the opportunities globalization provides. In other words: blame the player, not the instrument!

Trade in commodities is unfair

Looking at the figures, it would seem that exporting primary commodities is no longer important for developing countries; in the year 2000 only 9 percent of developing country merchandise exports were made up of foodstuffs, agricultural raw materials made up 2 percent and metals another 4 percent. In 2001, fuels accounted for 21 percent and manufactures for 61 percent! However, if we were to look at the composition of the export products of individual developing countries, the picture is quite different. Thirty-seven Highly Indebted Poor Countries (HIPC) obtain more than half of their merchandise exports from primary products. In Sub-Saharan Africa, seventeen countries obtain 75 percent or even more of their export earnings from non-oil commodity exports. As already mentioned, commodity prices have fallen far below the levels of two decades ago. Thanks to China's enormous demand for raw materials, prices are temporarily going up again. Yet, price volatility will remain. The demand for most products is more or less fixed. It is unlikely, for instance, that the global demand for coffee will grow dramatically in the foreseeable future. Moreover, some raw materials (e.g., jute, rubber and copper) have been replaced by cheaper man-made product alternatives.

What can be done to improve the situation of those developing countries still dependent on exports of primary commodities? Supply reduction could be an option. However, where tried it failed for political or other reasons. Unfortunately, the *fair-trade movement* is hardly a solution: less than 1 percent of cocoa, tea and coffee sales are carried out on a fair-trade basis. There are other major obstacles as well. One is the *tariff escalation* applied by rich countries to prevent primary commodity exporters from processing their own products, and thus adding value themselves. This type of unacceptable discrimination ought to be taken up by the WTO as soon as possible. Another obstacle is the concentration of commodity trade in just a few hands: Nestlé and Philip Morris, for example, control half the market share of roasted and instant coffee. The sad conclusion is that it is better not to only rely on primary commodities for one's exports, but to diversify exports as soon as possible.

The WTO, a hated symbol of globalization

In the eyes of its opponents, the WTO serves only the interests of rich countries; it is undemocratic and demonstrates no transparency in its decision-making processes. The WTO is in fact an institutional response to a practical problem: how to sustain a mutually beneficial liberal economy in a world of many sovereign states of vastly different economic strength and sophistication, all of which are subject to protectionist pressures. In other words, the WTO helps to provide the international public good of open markets. In the past this was provided by large economies such as the United States and the European Union. They entered into reciprocal commitments to liberalize trade whose benefits have been spread worldwide through the principle of non-discrimination, supported by WTO's predecessor, the General Agreement on Tariffs and Trade (GATT).

The WTO does not do away with the inequality in the power of nations. True, the big players have more clout than smaller ones. The WTO is not a system of global government, but rather a way of organizing and disciplining the unequal capacity for self-help of member-states. At present, the WTO works on the basis of a consensus among states, with the biggest and most economically significant having the largest influence. If, for instance, the "one man one vote" system were to be introduced, India and China would command 40 percent of the votes, and this in turn would not reflect their actual weight in international trade.

What could be done is to help developing country governments and their private sectors to be better involved in the WTO; donor countries should help them achieve this. At any event, at the last meeting at Doha, the developing countries insisted that if another round of trade negotiations was to be initiated, their concerns had to be better heard – and they achieved some concession. With China joining the WTO, developing countries have a powerful voice on their side – though the interests of China and those of many poor developing countries, in particular, do not necessarily coincide.

A suggestion would be to consider whether developing countries should have greater freedom to introduce export conditions, export subsidization and any other instrument to promote their early stage of industrialization, in line with Ha-Joon Chang's analysis. Also, to force developing countries to adopt OECD quality environmental standards through trade threats would be an abuse of power by the industrial countries – it would be a form of taxation on poor countries: the opposite of development assistance, so to speak!

The WTO offers poor countries their best prospect of forcing powerful countries to adhere to international rules. Without the WTO the big powers might do what they want to an even greater extent than they already do, and that is not what even the opponents of the WTO want!

All in all, the complaints against the WTO are exaggerated. It is not a closed shop, it is not undemocratic; in fact WTO's secretariat is weak and understaffed. It can and should be strengthened and improved, as there is no better alternative in sight to provide the international public good of open markets, especially now that the Doha Round has to be brought to a satisfactory conclusion.

Hypocritical high-income countries

If anything, here the critics have a valid point in claiming that the rich countries are hypocritical in their treatment of developing countries. They handicap the world's poor countries with obstacles to trade far bigger than those they impose on one another. In general, the United States, Canada, the European Union, and Japan charge far higher tariffs (including tariff peaks exceeding 15 percent) than their average tariff (3 percent) for labor-intensive manufactured imports (such as clothing and shoes) and for processed foodstuffs. Unfortunately, developing countries are also damaged by the protectionism of *other* developing countries. The World Bank has calculated that the average tariff faced by the poor (i.e., those living on 2 USD a day, at PPP) in all markets is 14 percent, against 6 percent for the rest of the world, as a result of barriers in both high-income countries and other developing countries.

The Progressive Policy Institute (PPI) provides examples of what these tariff implications are for poor countries. Exports to the US from Bangladesh, with a GDP per head of USD 370, paid USD 331 million in tariffs in 2001, or an average rate of 14.1 percent. This revenue was as big as that levied on exports from France. But French exports were thirteen times greater, so the average rate they paid was only 1.1 percent. Similarly, exports from Cambodia, with a GDP per head of USD 260 paid USD 152 million in tariffs, an average rate of 15.8 percent, while Singapore's exports paid USD 96 million, an average rate of only 0.6 percent. The PPI concluded that the world's least developed countries face tariffs four or five times higher than the richest economies[72]. This is grossly unfair and absolutely unacceptable!

Tariff escalation applied by rich countries was already mentioned on page 68. This is especially true for the EU and Japan. On average, the tariff in the EU on processed commodities is 2.75 times higher than that on unprocessed commodities. In Japan, the ratio is 3.75. Such escalation makes protection to domestic value added vastly higher than one realizes. This probably explains why the UK and Holland, for example, still process and sell enormous quantities of cocoa, tea and coffee. Anti-dumping and preferential trading arrangements also do not help improve the trading position of poor countries. Bangladesh, for example, is excluded from any preferential trading arrangements. These arrangements may form an obstacle to further overall trade liberalization, as the beneficiaries may well wish to defend their preferences.

The best known, and ongoing, scandal concerns the subsidies of agricultural products within the EU. According to the OECD, total assistance to rich country farmers was USD 311 billion in 2001, six times as much as all development assistance, and more than the entire GDP of Sub-Saharan Africa. In 2000, the EU provided USD 913 per cow raised in EU countries and USD 8 to each Sub-Saharan African. The Japanese, more generous still, although only to cows, provided USD 2,700 for each of their cows, and just USD 1.47 to each African person.

Because these farm subsidies are anti-cyclical, they increase the instability of residual world markets, with devastating effects on exporters from developing countries. Moreover, subsidized surpluses are still being dumped on world markets. The EU is the world's largest exporter of skimmed milk powder, at half the costs of production. It is also the largest exporter of white sugar, at a quarter of the cost of production. It is obvious that developing countries would gain enormously from the elimination of the subsidies as mentioned above[73]. The World Bank has estimated the annual welfare losses to developing countries at USD 20 billion per year, close to 40 percent of all development assistance.

Then, there is the topic of trade related *intellectual property rights*. This aspect was included in the Uruguay Round negotiations and forms part of the WTO. This may be beneficial to large developing countries such as Brazil, India, and China; the smaller ones only pay the price, with potentially devastating effects for their ability to educate their people (because of copyrights), adapt designs for their own use (also copyrights) and deal with the severe challenges of public health. As for this last-mentioned aspect, due to international outrage, the drug companies were forced to provide AIDS-retarding medicines to South Africa. As Stiglitz noted: "No one denies the importance of intellectual property rights. But these rights need to balance the rights and interests of producers against those of users, not only users in developing countries but also researchers in developed countries"[74].

Again, the World Bank estimated that transfers from developing countries in the form of license payments to transnational companies will rise almost four-fold in the coming years from their current level of USD 15 billion, thus outnumbering the total amount of development assistance. Furthermore, there is *bio-piracy*, meaning that international companies are patenting traditional medicines and foods. By doing so they squelch domestic firms that have long provided these products.

While the developed countries preach the virtues of competitive markets to developing countries, they continue to give their own farmers billions of dollars in subsidies, and protect their steel and aluminum producers, making it impossible for the developing countries to compete. All in all, in this realm, the rich countries treat the developing countries badly and hypocritically. Further trade liberalization should benefit everybody, especially the poor developing countries. With the necessary political will and common sense it can be done, and not only will the developing countries gain, everyone will.

Taking a closer look at globalization's effects

So far we dealt with globalization in broad terms: 3 billion bene-fited; 2 billion people did not (as yet). There are many authors who apply a finer analytical scalpel to lay bare globalization's winners and losers. Two interesting views are presented in this section: Geoffrey Garrett's as reflected in: *Globalization's Missing Middle*[75], and Amy Chua's, as presented in her highly successful book: *World on Fire*[76].

Geoffrey Garrett maintains that globalization has squeezed the middle-class, both within societies and in the international system. And as for countries, he writes that middle-income countries have not done nearly as well in globalized markets as the rich or poorer countries. Worse still, those middle-income countries that opened up their markets fared especially badly. Why is that? Because they have not been able to find a particular *niche* in world markets. They have been unable to compete in high value-added markets domi-nated by the rich economies because their work forces are not sufficiently skilled and their legal and banking systems are not sophisticated enough. As a result, they have had little choice but to try to compete with China and other low-income countries in markets for standardized products made with widely available and relatively old technologies. But because of their higher wages, the middle-income countries are bound to lose that battle. Garrett mainly uses Latin American economies as examples for his thesis. These economies have work forces that are not skilled enough, and their economic institutions are not sufficiently supportive of investment or innovation to take advantage of the knowledge workers they do have.

The problem with Garrett's article is that he provides little statisti-cal evidence, so it is hard to confirm or refute what he presents. Moreover, he relates openness – in some instances – almost directly with performance. For example, he notes that those Latin American countries that cut their tariffs most grew the slowest. However, there are many more factors that may explain this performance. What should be done to improve their performance? Garrett includes the following factors in his advice for improvement, which are not much different from the New Institutional Economics school recipe: meaningful educational reform is long overdue in these countries, as are institutional reforms in government, banking and law, which could transform economies that stifle innovation into ones that foster it, with strong property-rights regimes, effective financial systems, and good governance.

The countries concerned cannot do this all by themselves, as it is too Herculean a task, says Garrett. Moreover, the transition to democracy in Latin America since the 1980s has raised popular expectations that politicians find increasingly difficult to satisfy. What the US and the EU must do to help Latin America, concludes Garrett, is to help develop – above all – knowledge economies.

Although Garrett mentions shortcomings in the functioning of Latin American economies (and that of other middle-income countries), one cannot escape from the impression that he puts a large part of the blame on globalization, and that solutions must come from the US and the EU. True, the rich countries do share a responsibility to ensure a more equitable distribution of economic wealth throughout the world, especially to promote stability and to help create a safer world. But what is often forgotten is that the prime responsibility lies with each individual country.

Many historical, political, economic, and cultural reasons can be put forward (which have nothing to do with globalization) to explain why Latin America is not benefiting from globalization as much as the rich countries and emerging economies do. Examples would be the snails pace of regional integration so as to enlarge internal markets, the negative effects of import-substitution policies, which prevented the building up of robust export-oriented industries (Latin America cannot boast of having any large multinational company), the Hispanic-indigenous mix which was not conducive to private sector development. Neither did the majority of the countries create an adequate educational system, nor a professional civil service and an independent Judiciary. It may be no surprise then that in environments like these, as Martin Wolf put it: "Very low standards of living have meant correspondingly limited ability to provide any of the necessary public goods that underpin economic growth. Education remains inadequate and illiteracy is rife. Economic activity remains extremely unsophisticated. Ambitious people view politics as a way to extract the wealth unavailable in normal economic activity. The result is corruption, or, at worst, civil war"[77]. To my mind this explains Latin America's failure to catch-up much better, despite almost 200 years of independence, than globalization.

Amy Chua wrote a well-documented book on some of the effects of globalization. In a nutshell the thesis of her book is that the global spread of markets and democracy is a principal aggravating cause of group hatred and ethnic violence throughout the non-Western world. Why is that? Because, according to Chua, markets concentrate enormous wealth in the hands of an outsider minority, fomenting ethnic envy and hatred among often chronically poor majorities. Chua provides a wealth of examples to underpin her thesis: Bolivia, Brazil, Cameroon, Indonesia, Kenya, Nigeria, her home country the Philippines, Rwanda, post-Communist Russia, Thailand, South-Africa, and so forth. Adolf Hitler, who in the1930s and 1940s had Jews persecuted and mass-murdered, already provided the cruelest example.

Chua describes the relevance of the rise of democracy – together with globalization – to support her central thesis, as follows: "As markets enrich the market-dominant minority, democratization increases the political voice and power of the frustrated majority"[78]. The version of capitalism being promoted outside the West today is essentially laissez-faire and rarely includes any significant redistributive mechanism, says Chua. To lessen the tensions, Chua advocates that poor and emerging economies apply redistributive policies such as investment in free education and health, social safety nets, and the like. Chua paradoxically concludes by saying that: "...the best hope for democratic capitalism in the non-Western world lies with market-dominant minorities themselves"[79]. When looking at the stagnant economies of Latin America, which I know best, I can only agree with Amy Chua. The only way to get out of stagnation is economic growth. For the various reasons provided above, it seems as though only entrepreneurial minorities demonstrate the drive to break the vicious circle, provided they are being supported by governments and societies that appreciate the beneficial political, social and economic effects of growth and development.

Conclusion

Overcoming poverty is probably the most pressing challenge the world faces today. Globalization can contribute greatly. The point is that those poor countries that have not yet benefited could and should be included. However, some obstacles have to be overcome, and development policies should be adjusted, so that the losers of today will belong to the winners of tomorrow. But, what should be done?

First, tariffs and other limiting factors in the free flow of goods and services should be further brought down, especially those tariffs that limit the export possibilities for poor developing countries. Second, the sky-high agricultural subsidies of the high-income countries should be reduced, if not abolished altogether, so as to do away with the huge welfare losses they imply for the world economy at large. Third, migration should not be limited by policies applied by the EU and the US, for example. Instead, it should be freed-up, as it helps bring down poverty in the migrants' home countries and contribute to further economic growth of the countries they migrate to. And, poor countries that have not already done so, should get their own economies in order so as to benefit from globalization. Macro-economic stability should be ensured, human resources should be developed, their investment climates should be made attractive for foreign direct investment – including the adherence to property rights – and government and the private sector should *together* design and implement policies that promote production, employment and export.

Friend and foe agree that, on balance, globalization contributes to the fight against poverty. Those countries that did not open themselves up still belong to the losers. This is troubling because poverty breeds discontent and instability. It also fosters terrorism[80]. Hence, there is not enough globalization; no, there is still too little. If all those poor countries still left out were to be included in the globalization process and benefit from it, the world would be a more decent, stable and peaceful place.

Bernard Shaw took three years to write his *Intelligent Woman's Guide*, declaring that only by addressing it to women could he shake off the academic style that makes political economy unreadable and remind himself continually to keep to the practical points that appeal to sensible women and repel male talkers. Should his sister-in-law have had any offspring of the female species, I do hope that she, given access to this essay, would have appreciated it.

References

Bhagwati, J., 2004: *In Defense of Globalization* (New York: Oxford University Press)

Cavenaugh, J., et al., 2002: *Alternative to Globalization: A Better World is Possible* (San Francisco: Barrett-Koehler)

Chua, A., 2004: *The World on Fire: How Exporting Free Market Democracy Breeds Ethnic Hatred and Global Instability* (New York: Random House)

Ferguson, N., 2005: *Sinking Globalization* (Foreign Affairs, March/April)

Fischer, S., 2003: *Globalization and its Challenges* (The Richard T. Ely Lecture)

Friedman, T., 2000: *The Lexus and the Olive Tree* (New York: Anchor Books)

Galbraith, J., 1979: *The Nature of Mass Poverty* (Hammondsworth: Penguin Books)

Garrett, G., 2004: *Globalization's Missing Middle* (Foreign Affairs, November/December)

Ha-Joon Chang, 2002: *Kicking Away the Ladder: Development Strategy in Historical Perspective* (London: Anthem Press)

Hoffmann, S., 2002: *Clash of Globalizations* (Foreign Affairs, July/August)

Lomborg, B., 2001: *The Skeptical Environmentalist: Measuring the Real State of the World* (Cambridge: Cambridge University Press)

Monbiot, G., 2003: *The Age of Consent: A Manifesto for a New World Order* (London: Harper Collins)

Pamuk, O., 2001: *The Anger of the Damned* (The New York Review of Books, November 15)

Progressive Policy Institute, 2002: *America's Hidden Tax on the Poor: The Case for Reforming US Tariff Policy* (Washington)

Rodrik, D., 1998: *The New Global Economy: Making Openness Work* (Baltimore: Johns Hopkins University Press, Policy Essay No. 24)

Sachs, J., 1999: *Latinoamérica y el Desarollo Económico Global* In: Toranzo, C., et.al. *Bolivia en el Siglo XX* (La Paz: Harvard Club de Bolivia)

Stiglitz, J., 2002: *Globalization and its Discontents* (London: Penguin Books)

The Economist, 2005: *A Survey of India and China* (Issue 5 March)

Williamson, J., 2002: *Winners and Losers over Two Centuries of Globalization* (Cambridge MA: National Bureau of Economic Research Working Paper)

World Bank, 2002: *Globalization, Growth and Poverty* (Washington: A World Bank Policy Research Report)

Wolf, M., 2004: *Why Globalization Works* (New Haven & London: Yale University Press)

State and Market in Development

Human institutions such as the state are not rational, but we can decide to fight to make them more rational. We ourselves and our ordinary language are, on the whole, emotional rather than rational; but we can try to become a little more rational, and we can train ourselves to use our language as an instrument not of self-expression ... but of rational communication;
... this civilization has not yet fully recovered from the shock of its birth – the transition from the tribal or "closed society" with its submission to magical forces, to the "open society" which sets free the critical powers of man.

K.R. Popper, *The Open Society and its Enemies* (1977)

Practical men, who believe themselves to be quite exempt from any intellectual influences, are usually the slaves of some defunct economist. Madmen in authority, who hear voices in the air, are distilling their frenzy from some academic scribbler of a few years back... soon or late, it is ideas, not vested interests, which are dangerous for good or ill.

J.M. Keynes, *The General Theory of Employment, Interest and Money* (1936)

We are accustomed to thinking of great cultural and social changes as occurring during times of military defeat or political breakdown. But nothing produces change more inevitably than growth, and growth in population, production, trade, culture, and institutions takes place more easily in peaceful times than during periods of disruption.

John K. Fairbank and Edwin O. Reischauer, *China, Tradition and Transformation* (1984)

Introduction

A society functions properly if government and the market each play their part efficiently and if their interrelationships are efficient and appropriate as well. These are the two basic ingredients for sustained economic development and for the fight against poverty.

There are only some twenty odd countries – mainly the OECD members – that thus far have achieved economic development over extended periods of time. The others are lagging behind and only a few amongst them are catching up. Perhaps Karl Popper was right when he concluded that civilization the world over has not yet overcome the shock of its birth, that is the transition from a traditional to a modern, open society.

Evidence shows that success in promoting economic growth and poverty reduction is most likely when governments complement markets; failures result when they conflict. When governments allow markets to function well, and when they concentrate their interventions on areas in which markets prove inadequate, positive results can be expected.

In this essay I deal with the economic role of the state and the question about the right mix between the role of the state and that of the market, followed by the presentation of a few theories on the functions of the state and the market. In my conclusion I address their respective roles in developing country contexts.

The economics perspective

What is the economic role of the state? The simple answer would be: to provide public goods, while the market provides private goods. This answer is particularly conditioned by the distinction between state and market. *The* distinguishing feature of the state is that its membership is universal, and that it has powers of compulsion not given to other organizations[81].

In purely economic terms, the price mechanism, or the working of a market economy, needs to be supplanted by various forms of direct government control, both national and international, to promote economic development. The essential task of government is seen as charting and implementing a strategy, thus providing the *incentives* for rapid and equitable growth. Free markets are neutral institutions, which can work for good or ill. Whatever may be said for their efficiency, they are not tenderhearted towards their victims. The question should focus on the conditions that can make markets "people-friendly". Certain conditions have to be met to make them work for the benefit of the people. There are several ways in which government intervention can contribute to a more efficient functioning of markets. Government should, for example, provide a legal framework and maintain law and order, including the enforcement of contracts, property rights, and so forth. It should pursue the correct macro-economic policies with respect to exchange rates and trade policy in order to ensure high levels of employment and economic growth.

What is the right mix?

Unfortunately, there is no standard recipe for the successful combined functioning of government and the market. Worse still, what the economic literature has proposed so far seems subject to *fads and fashions*. The thinking is cyclical: at times the role of government is paramount, then followed by an embracement of the blessings of the functioning of the free market[82]. The rise of neo-classical thinking in the early 1980s, for example, diminished the role of the state.

Advances in technology and telecommunications pressed on, shrinking distances, eroding national boundaries, ushering in *globalization*[83]. Increasingly, so it seems, these changes rendered governments mere servants of international markets. The collapse of communism at the end of the 1980s did not help to reverse the notion of the retreating state; 1989 did for "big" governments what 1929 did for laissez-faire. This is what The Economist had to say on the varying opinions on the role of the state versus that of the market: "In one corner are the optimists: an alliance of modernizing conservatives and the new post-socialist left. They regard the triumph of international capitalism largely as a good thing. Governments may have lost some of their freedom to direct economies as they wish, but the world is benefiting from faster technological progress, historically unprecedented opportunities for the relief of global poverty, and greater freedom for millions of people across the globe. Few optimists doubt that a well-functioning society requires a state that is competent in both senses of the word, which makes the state's shrinking economic sovereignty something of a drawback... The pessimists – a coalition of populist conservatives and the old left – agree on the need for a balance between an effective state and the economic efficiency that market forces can provide. They also agree that market forces have lately gained the upper hand. But unlike the optimists, the pessimists find this deeply disturbing. In their view, the gains from globalization are far smaller than the optimists suppose, and the drawbacks much greater. And such benefits as there may be will be divided unfairly within society – a crucial point that the optimists tend to ignore"[84].

Recent developments

World recession has followed the prosperous 1990s. The benefits of the free functioning of the market and of globalization have been put in doubt. The *Washington Consensus* is swaying on its foundations. It seems as if a *paradigm shift* is in the offing. This would imply a re-appreciation of the role of the state at the cost of the market.

Jorge Castañeda had this to say on this topic in relation to Latin America's stagnation: "Many in the region today believe that the main obstacles to growth are neither the weakness of economic reforms (essentially the conservative view) nor the nature of the reforms themselves (the left's perspective) but rather the poor quality of governmental institutions and corporate practices.

Reforming both is perhaps the region's greatest challenge – and last opportunity – to return to growth"[85].

Theories on the State

There is a whole menu of state theories to choose from. I will briefly describe below what I consider to be the more interesting ones.

Adam Smith, the father of modern economics, is often portrayed as the champion of "laissez faire"; meaning, the free functioning of the market. The Invisible Hand would make sure that an optimum situation results for society. However, Smith thought that the state should undertake three main tasks *(the duties of the King)*: (i) defending its citizens from the violence and invasion of other independent societies; (ii) protecting every member of society from the injustice or oppression of every other member of it; and (iii) erecting and maintaining certain public works and public institutions, the erecting and maintaining of which can never be in the interest of any individual or small number of individuals, because the profit would never repay the outlay, though it may frequently do much more than repay it to the great of society. Adam Smith also extensively discussed the importance of social interdependence and the communal advantages of following rules of conduct, even when they go against what he called "self love".

Modern theories, and developments since, have added justifications for large state intervention. In this vein, theoreticians like Pigou, Tinbergen and Meade assume that the state reigns above particular interests and conflicts and solely promotes the common good. According to this Platonic idea the state can do no wrong[86].

A vehement opponent of a large role of the state is Deepak Lal. He calls this large state intervention the Dirigiste Dogma. Lal says: "the essential elements of this dogma can be briefly stated. The major one is the belief that the price mechanism, or the working of a market economy, needs to be supplanted by various forms of direct government control, both national and international, to promote economic development... The essential task of governments is seen as charting and implementing a strategy for rapid and equitable growth which attaches prime importance to macro-economic accounting aggregates... The third element is the belief that the classical 19th century liberal case for free trade is invalid for developing countries, and thus government restriction of international trade and payments is necessary for development. Finally, it is believed that, to alleviate poverty and improve domestic income distribution, massive and continuing government intervention is required to redistribute assets and to manipulate the returns to different types of labor and capital through pervasive price and (if possible) wage controls... so that scarce resources are used to meet the so-called 'basic needs' of the poor rather than the luxurious 'wants' of the rich"[87].

There is another variety of thinkers that see little merit in the role of the state and its interventions. The neo-classical Chicago economists, neo-classical political economists and the public choice school of thought basically hold that government can do no right. Citizens, politicians, bureaucrats and states use the authority of government to distort economic transactions for their own benefit. Citizens use political influence and pressure to get access to benefits allocated by government; politicians use government resources to increase their hold on power; public officials trade access to government benefits for personal reward; and states use their power to get access to the property of citizens. The result is an inefficient and inequitable allocation of resources, general impoverishment and reduced freedom. This bleak picture is characterized by the term: *predatory state*. Any intervention by this predatory state with the "magic of the market place" is bound to make matters worse. Some countries give the impression that their citizens have entered into an anti-social contract with their governments: we shall not pay taxes, and in return we do not expect any public services.

Comparing the Platonic and the – seemingly opposite – public choice view, both conclude that the state is an optimizing agency. According to the Platonic view it optimizes the welfare of the people as a whole. From the public choice view, the welfare of special interest groups optimizes: those on whose support the politicians rely, the bureaucrats, the army and the politicians themselves. The Platonic view, as already mentioned, is normative; the public choice view is crudely cynical.

Michael Oakeshott, a philosopher and historian, described two ideas of government that have been in contention for centuries[88]. The first, rooted in ancient Greece, is the state as *civil association*. From this view, the state's job is to help people live their own lives according to their own ideas, imposing no goals of its own on its citizens. In contrast with that is the idea of the state as *enterprise association*. From this view, the state has aims of its own (to raise the incomes of all its subjects, say, to establish economic equality among them, to conquer neighboring lands, to glorify God): government directs the enterprise in order to achieve these goals. The first view puts individuals at the center, the second society. From the first view comes classical liberalism, and from that, amongst others, the Constitution of the United States. From the second comes socialism, and many varieties of modern conservatism. It is still an open question as to whether once a market economy is established it can be maintained against the unavoidable political pressures for its subversion. The notion that the pendulum is swinging back from too much reliance on markets to a more profound appreciation of the role of the state only shows how entrenched the idea of the state as an enterprise association has become.

Not losing sight of the real world

Theories are one way of looking at problems; empirical evidence is another[89]. Let us look at what really happened to the role and – above all – the *size* of governments in the course of time. Did they grow and shrink as a response to economic and political circumstances as some theories suggest? The answer is no! Big government is not dead; it is very much alive and kicking. Since the beginning of last century the industrial nations government's share of the economy moved in one direction only: up. Among the rich industrial countries, America and Japan have the smallest governments. In 1996, their public spending was 33 percent and 36 percent of GDP, respectively. In America, government spending in 1913 accounted for less than 2 percent of the economy, by 1937 it was still only 9 percent. America's government has grown by about a fifth since 1960. Internationally, the average increase over that period was more than three-fifths, while public spending in Japan more than doubled.

The point is that despite fierce pro-market policies as applied by Ronald Reagan, for instance, government budgets have steadily grown instead of diminishing. Why is that? Let us first look at the main components of governments' budgets. They are: (i) transfers and subsidies; (ii) government consumption, measured by what the state, as a supplier of services spends on wages and other inputs; (iii) interest; and (iv) public investment. What we see over the years – especially after 1960 – is a dramatic increase in transfers and subsidies, such as social security transfers and pensions. Altogether the cash-in-hand sector of the modern welfare state has, on average, grown to take up a quarter of the economy. The *wage bill* and other inputs are also on the increase and so is interest on governments' debts. Only public investment is decreasing. Deficits have become more or less permanent. This is a sign that governments are persistently spending more than their citizens can be persuaded to pay in taxes. Spending on consumption (that is, on services such as defense, education, law and order and health) has risen substantially.

Deadweight

This would seem to suggest an enormous rise in the quantity and quality of the services provided. But, alas, this is not so. The public sector has the unfortunate characteristic that its level of productivity rises much more slowly than in private business. A good part of the enormous increase in resources devoted to public services can be explained by that slow-rising productivity.

Moreover, increasing taxes, as practice has shown, have a *deadweight cost*. The bigger the government, the larger the influence of diminishing returns. At low levels of government activity, the deadweight cost of taxes may well be outweighed by the gains that flow from essential public goods. But as the scale of government grows, this trade-off seems likely to move into the wrong direction and at an accelerating pace.

On the spending side, further inefficiencies of various kinds arise often because government is usually a monopolistic provider of the services it supplies. This is either because it forbids competition, or because its services are "free" to users. Moreover, a public monopolist is free from pressures to innovate or become more efficient.

In conclusion, the deadweight costs of taxes, together with the inefficiencies caused by lack of competition and proper incentives within the public sector, helps to explain why government begins to fail as it grows.

Value for money

The big question is: does the population of big governments, as opposed to small governments, get value for their (tax) money? Let us go back to the 1960s when the dramatic increase in government spending really took off. Before the 1960s a much larger share of public spending was devoted to dealing with genuine market failures, as they would now be called. After that, the state expanded its role by seizing and monopolizing activities hitherto left to the market. As a result, in recent decades the connection between increased public spending and improved social outcomes has become much weaker.

Let us compare the performance of big government countries (public spending accounts for more than 50 percent of output) such as

Belgium, Sweden, Norway, the Netherlands, and small government ones (less than 35 percent of output), such as Australia, Hong Kong, Japan, Singapore, Switzerland, and the US. Between them, performance in average income, economic growth and health do not differ much. In education, the small government countries did markedly better, on average, than the big government countries, particularly in math. There was one aspect in which the big government countries did much better, and that was regarding inequality of incomes. In the big government countries, the poorest 20 percent of the population receive 7.4 percent of the national income, whilst in the small government ones they get only 5.6 percent. Conversely, the richest 20 percent were much better off in the small government countries than in the big ones, both in absolute terms and relative to the less prosperous in their own economies.

This comparison begs the question as to whether this modest increase in equality justifies surrendering an extra 15-20 percent of the economy to public control. Today's fastest growing emerging market economies have much smaller governments than most of their western counterparts did at comparable stages of their development. Two of the Asian Tigers have already surpassed the incomes the West had achieved by 1960. Others are getting there fast, with governments smaller than America's was 40 years ago. In years to come, the question is: will the Asian Tigers build welfare states of their own and if so, will they be able to maintain their faster rates of growth? This question is even more pertinent now that the erstwhile star grower Singapore, for instance, is having difficulties sustaining its growth rate[90].

Although the above comparison may be compelling, I believe a more thorough analysis is required before drawing final conclusions. One observation would be that it is apparently very costly to achieve redistribution of incomes. Second, the better offs in the economy of big government countries are more prepared to share some of their wealth, via taxes, with the poorer sections of society. Third, there is the aspect of social upward mobility. It seems to me that not only *access* to education but also its *affordability* are both vital conditions to move upward in social and economic life. Are these conditions really the same for the poorer sections of small government societies? I doubt it. If we were to take the example of the US, there is a wide gap in income between the rich and the poor, and the respective levels of educational attainment explain this gap to a large extent. Then, at least three of the small government countries are federal governments, leaving a lot of public service delivery to the states (US, Australia) and cantons (Switzerland). This may lead to an incorrect reflection of the *actual* (higher) level of their respective public spending. All the same, the challenge for big government countries is to dramatically bring the deadweight costs of their public services down, by improving their efficiency and effectiveness.

Will the nation-state survive globalization?

As labor and capital become more mobile, governments will be drawn into competition with each other, and – all things being equal – the effects of this competition will be to roll back the state. Some scholars suggest that states will, like firms in comparable circumstances, form cartels. The idea is that governments are pooling power in order to retain it. The European Union (EU) and the North American Free Trade Agreement (NAFTA) form examples of this trend. So far, as empirical evidence shows, the states' freedom of action has been barely touched by the global market. However, should it become more circumscribed, a growing trend towards more rule by a cartel can be expected.

Martin Wolf, associate editor of the Financial Times, maintains that globalization will not spell the end of the modern nation-state[91]. Wolf explains that the present wave of globalization is not much different from the first one, around the turn of the nineteenth century. The difference with the present wave of globalization lies in the advances in technology and infrastructure, which substantially reduced the costs of transportation and communications. But it is not these two factors that basically drive integration of markets. It is *policy* that has determined the extent and pace of international economic integration. For, if transport and communications innovations were moving toward global integration over the past century and a half, policy was clearly not. For this reason, the growth in the potential for economic integration has greatly outpaced the growth of integration itself since the late nineteenth century. Globalization has much further to go, that is, if it is allowed to do so.

Globalization is often perceived as destructive to governments' capacities to do what they want or need, particularly in the key areas of taxation, public spending and macro-economic policy. But how true is this perception? First, taxation. Evidence reveals that taxation within OECD countries went up instead of down since the integration of international markets. It is electoral resistance and not globalization that has most significantly limited the growth of taxation. True, collecting taxes is becoming harder for various reasons, such as the mobility of labor, cross-border shopping, electronic commerce and the expansion of tax havens. Governments are indeed forming cartels to halt these developments, which they see as ruinous competition for taxation. However, one of the most intriguing phenomena of modern Europe is that high-tax, big-spending Scandinavian countries are leading the new economy! Skilled Scandinavians are not leaving their countries by the thousands. They still pay their taxes and enjoy high-quality schools or public transport. Competition among governments will not be eliminated, because the powerful countries that provide relatively low-tax, low-spending environments will want to maintain them. All in all, governments will be increasingly forced to provide value for money for those who pay for their services.

The assumption that most governments are Platonian benevolent welfare-maximizers is, as we have already seen, naïve. International economic integration creates competition among governments; even countries that fiercely resist integration cannot survive in uncompetitive economies. This competition constrains the ability of governments to act in a predatory manner and increases the *incentive* to provide services that are valued by those who pay taxes.

The proposition that globalization makes states unnecessary is simply wrong. First, the ability of a society to take advantage of the opportunities offered by international economic integration depends on the quality of public goods, such as property rights, an honest and professional civil service, personal security and high quality of, especially higher, education. Second, international governance rests on the ability of individual states to provide and guarantee stability. The bedrock of international order is the territorial state with, as Max Weber already stated, a monopoly on coercive power within its jurisdiction. Globalization does not make states unnecessary. On the contrary, for people to be successful in exploiting the opportunities afforded by international integration, they need states at both ends of the transactions. Failed states, disorderly states, predatory states, and corrupt states are shunned as the black holes of the global economic system.

The market

It is difficult to imagine that any process of development can do without the extensive use of markets. However, this does not preclude the role of social support, public regulation, or statecraft when they enrich – rather than impoverish – societies. Nobel Laureate Amartya Sen says that *freedom* is the principal end of development: "The contribution of the market mechanism to economic growth is, of course, important, but this comes only after the direct significance of the freedom to interchange...has been acknowledged"[92].

In assessing the market mechanism, it is important to distinguish between various types of markets, whether competitive or monopolistic (or otherwise uncompetitive), whether some markets may be missing, and so forth. Also the nature of factual circumstances (such as the availability or absence of information, the presence or absence of economies of scale) may influence the actual possibilities to impose real limitations on what can be achieved through the market mechanism. The major cause of incomplete markets is imperfect information, which causes the problem of what is called "incentive compatibility". In the absence of such imperfections, classical models of general equilibrium have been used to demonstrate the merits of the market mechanism in achieving economic efficiency, otherwise known as the *Pareto optimum*: a situation in which the utility (or welfare) of one person cannot be raised without reducing the utility (or welfare) of someone else.

The role that markets play must depend not only on what they can do, but also on what they are allowed to do. There are many people whose interests are well served by the smooth functioning of the markets, but there are also groups whose established interests may be hurt by such functioning. If the latter groups are politically more powerful and influential, they can try to see that markets are not given adequate room in the economy. This can be a particularly serious problem when monopolistic production units flourish despite inefficiency and various types of ineptitude due to insulation from competition, either domestic or foreign. The high product prices or low product qualities that are involved in such artificially propped up production may impose significant sacrifice on the population at large, but an organized and politically influential group of industrialists can make sure that their profits are well protected. Adam Smith has already complained about the detrimental influence of vested interests in guaranteeing the insulation of their inflated profits from the threatening effects of competition. These pre-capitalist constraints are quite representative of the restrictions that frustrate the functioning of economies of many developing countries.

Limits of the market

A main problem of markets is that not everybody has the same access to them. Not everybody has enough financial resources to buy goods and services. The equity problems have to be addressed, especially dealing with serious deprivation and poverty. Government has an important role in countering this dismal situation.

This is what social security systems in welfare states try to achieve. But the need to pay attention simultaneously to efficiency and equity motivates interference with the working of the market mechanism that can weaken efficiency achievements even if it promotes equity. An example would be the greater social commitment in Europe (more than in the United Sates) in guaranteeing minimal incomes and health care, with a greater commitment in the United States (more than in Europe) in maintaining high levels of employment. To the extent that there is a conflict, the need for simultaneity in considering the two issues would be important in arriving at overall social priorities.

The market can play a very useful role in furthering the well being of society. Yet, it is not the best and only solution for every economic challenge, such as the overall development of a society and the fight against poverty. What are the limits of the market? The equity issue has already been mentioned. The market mechanism needs to be supplemented with other activities, such as social security provisions. The market mechanism may sometimes be less effective, particularly in the provision of public goods, such as basic education and health, as the market's rationale is geared to private goods.

There are also mixed cases. For example, given the shared communal benefits of basic education, which may transcend the gains of the person being educated, basic education may have a public-good component as well (and can thus be seen as a semi-public good). The persons receiving education do, of course, benefit from it, but in addition a general expansion of education and literacy in a region can facilitate social change and also help to promote economic progress from which others benefit too. The state has typically played a major role in the expansion of basic education. The rapid spread of literacy in the history of the rich countries of today has drawn on the low cost of public education combined with its shared public benefits. In this context it is rather remarkable that some market enthusiasts now recommend to developing countries that they should rely fully on the free market even for basic education, thereby withholding from them the very process of educational expansion that was crucial to the rapid spread of literacy in Europe, North America, Japan and, more recently, the Asian Tigers.

Conclusion

The market mechanism is a vital arrangement through which people can interact with each other and undertake mutually beneficial activities. In this perspective, it is hard indeed to see how any reasonable critic could be against the market mechanism, as such. The problems that arise spring typically from other sources – not from the existence of markets per se – and include such concerns as inadequate preparedness to make use of market transactions, unconstrained concealment of information or unregulated use of activities that allow the powerful to capitalize on their asymmetrical advantage. These have to be dealt with not by suppressing the markets, but by allowing them to function better and with greater fairness, and with adequate supervision. The overall achievements of the market are deeply contingent on political and social arrangements.

The market mechanism has achieved great success under those conditions in which the opportunities offered by them could be reasonably shared. In making this possible, the provision of basic education, the presence of elementary medical facilities, and the availability of resources (such as land) that can be crucial to some economic activities, call for appropriate public policies. Even when the need for economic reform in favor of allowing more room for markets is paramount, these non-market facilities require careful and determined public action. The far-reaching powers of the market mechanism have to be supplemented by the creation of basic social opportunities for social equity and justice. And this is particularly vital for developing countries. However, investments in social development, such as health and education for the poor, should go hand in hand with a sound policy to promote economic growth. Unfortunately, quite a few developing countries make strides in the former, without them being translated into economic improvement of the poor.

Human development is not a luxury that can only be afforded by rich countries. Perhaps the most important impact of the type of success that the East Asian economies have recently had (beginning with Japan) is the total undermining of this prejudice. These economies went comparatively early for massive expansion of education, and later also of health-care, and this they did, in many cases, *before* they broke the restraints of general poverty. Indeed, the priority of human resource development applies particularly to the early history of Japanese economic development, beginning with the Meji Restauration in the mid-nineteenth century. Surely, human development is – first and foremost – an ally of the poor!

The role of the state in developing countries

So far I have been dealing with the role of the state from a normative, theoretical point of view, while mainly referring to its role in the industrialized world. This section deals with the role of the state in the context of a developing country.

Let me quote Deepak Lal again: "...anyone familiar with the actual administration and implementation of policies in many Third World countries, and not blinkered by the Dirigiste Dogma, should find that oft-neglected work, *The Wealth of Nations*, both so relevant and so modern. For in most of our modern-day equivalents of the inefficient 18th-century state, not even the minimum governmental functions required for economic progress are always fulfilled. Yet the dirigists have been urging a myriad of new tasks on Third World governments, which go well beyond what Keynes, considered as being a sensible agenda for mid-20th-Century Western polities'[93].

Although Lal's style is amusing and polemic, he very rightly draws attention to the inappropriate and unjustified projection of a welfare state model (to counter market imperfections) onto developing countries, many of whom had just gained independence, and were thus in no position whatsoever to provide public services that could possibly handle not only the day to day affairs of government, but also promote economic development in combination with the provision of a wide range of social goods and services. Yet, this is what the overwhelming majority of development economists prescribed from the 1950s to the late 1970s. No wonder that after the second oil crisis of 1979 many governments of developing countries nearly collapsed.

There were only very few development thinkers, such as Peter Bauer[94], who opposed the dirigist development prescription. In hindsight, betting especially on the state to promote development was indeed a grave error. And so were many more prescriptions by development economists, such as import substitution, as promoted by Raul Prebisch, which did do a lot of harm to Latin America's development.

But what about an appropriate role of the state in a developing country environment? Merilee Grindle puts the role of the state in its historical perspective, after which she makes interesting proposals for the future in her *Challenging the State*[95]. Her discourse is as follows. The economic crisis of the late 1970s and the early 1980s greatly undermined the capacity of developing country states to encourage economic development and maintain social stability. During that time *government failures* (meaning, the way in which public action can distort markets and create disincentives for productive investments) became painfully clear. Moreover, many governments had expanded the numbers of civil servants to unsustainable proportions. Politicians had misused their position to provide jobs to their supporters and/or (extended) family members, not primarily on the basis of their *merits*, but on patron-client criteria.

The effects of the second oil crisis triggered a new orthodoxy of market liberalism with a strong anti-state bias. To many development economists the notion of a *minimalist state* replaced that of the *developmentalist* state. But the minimalists carried their argument too far. By the late 1980s a re-appreciation of the role of the state came about (namely, re-inventing government!), amongst others as a consequence of the steep decline in social service delivery, which hit the poor hardest in developing countries. After all, states were important in the process of development because they alone could provide a set of conditions essential to economic development: law, order, effective macro-economic policies, infrastructure development, investment in human capital and the enhancement of equity.

The New Institutional Economics (NIE) demonstrated that western capitalist economies developed thanks to *institutional innovations* to ensure the rights of private accumulation and the sanctity of contracts among economic agents[96]. Increasingly, analysts emphasized the importance of the type and *quality* of state intervention rather than its quantity. Attention was also given, in this context, to the East Asian success stories. Actions and policies of development-oriented states in the Asian Tiger countries were central to generating high and sustained growth rates. In several of these countries strong, centralized interventionist and authoritarian states were specifically credited with engineering economic growth through state policies for investment, trade and social control. Thus, state capacity to set institutional structures conducive to economic growth, to manage macro-economic policy, and to carry out basic public functions, became important in explaining the differential history of states that developed as opposed to states that stagnated economically.

In the latter ones public service delivery deteriorated. Also the widespread phenomenon of corruption was identified as an eroding factor affecting not only the state's functioning, but also the rapidly worsening population's perception of the state. Especially in Africa and Latin America the credibility of the state deteriorated. This led to a disengagement from the state whereby individuals and groups withdrew or tried to avoid contact with officials and organizations representing it.

Governance

In a response to this disturbing development, political scientists argued that *capable states* had to be responsive to the demands and pressures of societal groups, to be able to mediate social demands and maintain institutions that were effective in resolving conflict. The concept of *governance*, referring in part to the political and institutional development of a country and its capacity to achieve and maintain good government, was increasingly used to denote a state's capacity to tolerate and even invite political pluralism. Grindle provides us with a clear description what a capable state would be: "A capable state is one that exhibits the ability to establish and maintain effective institutional, technical, administrative and political functions. Theoretically, states that exhibit these characteristics should be well equipped to manage tasks essential to economic and political development"[97]. Grindle basically defines a middle-ground role for the state, neither minimalist nor maximalist. At any rate, developing countries simply cannot afford a welfare state type as we see in most industrialized countries.

Technically speaking a state should have: (i) the ability to set and manage effective macro-economic policies; (ii) a cadre of well-trained economic analysts and managers; (iii) well-staffed and appropriately placed units for policy analysis; and (iv) an important role for technical input and information in decision-making. A capable state with adequate administrative capacity implies effective administration of basic physical and social infrastructure. And the ability to perform basic administrative functions is essential to economic development and social welfare. Then, its political capacity. The capable state should have effective and legitimate channels for societal demands, representation of societal interests, and conflict resolution. Responsive political leaders and administrators also belong to these requirements. Lastly, society should be able to participate in decision-making.

All this sounds fine, but it is a normative wish list which is hard to come by in a typical developing country context. Grindle admits that the economic crisis combined with increased political challenges to existing regimes weakened the legitimacy and coercive capacity of state institutions and laid bare the inadequacy of systems for regulating property rights, enforcing contracts, controlling corruption, setting boundaries on the use of coercion and other basic institutional functions. Paradoxically, experience over the past two decades shows that poor country governments' technical capacity to manage macro-economic policies and analyze policy options improved. The pressures of economic crisis prompted the need to negotiate more effectively with institutions such as the International Monetary Fund (IMF) and the World Bank. Ministries of Finance, Central Banks and national planning institutes became more powerful during the past 20 years. Contrary to the technical capacity, the state's administrative capacity declined during this period as a result of austerity budgets, declining civil service performance and heightened political conflict.

In conclusion, after decades of crisis, many governments may have increased their abilities in macro-economic management while losing valuable capacity to respond to public needs, develop human resources, maintain investment, and provide essential sectoral and infrastructural services. The question is, therefore, how should and could these wanting capacities be addressed[98]. The answer implies a redefinition of the relationship between the state and the market, as well as with civil society. It is especially in times of crisis that changes can and must be forged.

The market in developing countries

It is entrepreneurs that look for niches in the market. They supply goods and services for which there is a market. There are entrepreneurs in all societies, but they seem to be successful in some and not in others. Economic growth and decline are often directly related to the success with which entrepreneurs operate. But is this so? An interesting study by William Baumol sheds a fresh light on the matter[99]. He states that the question as to how the entrepreneur acts at a given time and place depends heavily on the *rules of the game* – the reward structure in the economy – that just happen to prevail. These determine whether entrepreneurship will be allocated in productive or unproductive directions, and that can significantly affect the vigor of the economy's productivity growth. When the rules of the game are conducive, innovation will be promoted and – in turn – entrepreneurs will put these innovations to productive use. When the rules of the game are not conducive, an entrepreneur may even lead a parasitical existence that is actually damaging to the economy[100]. Unfortunately, examples of this *unproductive entrepreneurship* can be found in many developing countries. Environments like these often accord a low social status to entrepreneurs and innovators.

This is not a recent phenomenon. No, it is as old as the world, so to speak. Finley, for instance, notes that the Roman reward system, although it offered wealth to those who engaged in commerce and industry, offset this gain through the attendant loss in prestige[101]. Economic effort... "was neither the way to wealth nor its purpose. Cato's gods showed him a number of ways to get more; but they were all political and parasitical, the ways of conquest and booty and usury; labor was not one of them, not even the labor of the entrepreneur"[102].

In China, if one was not a member of the mandarin class, the path to wealth was via the Confucian examination system, which provided the wished for social and economic mobility. Wealth was thus a prospect for those who passed the examination and who were subsequently appointed to government positions. But the *sources* of their earnings had something in common with those of the Romans: "Corruption, which is widespread in all impoverished and backward countries (or more exactly, throughout the pre-industrial world), was endemic in a country where the servants of the state often had nothing to live on but their very meager salaries. The required attitude of obedience to superiors made it impossible for officials to demand higher salaries, and in the absence of any control over their activities from below, it was inevitable that they should purloin from society what the state failed to provide. According to the usual pattern, a Chinese official entered upon his duties only after spending long years in study and passing many examinations; he then established relations with protectors, incurred debts to get himself appointed, and then proceeded to extract the amount he had spent on preparing himself for his career from the people he administered – and extracted both principal and interest. The degree of this rapacity would be dictated not only by the length of time he had had to wait for his appointment and the number of relations he had to support and of kin to satisfy or repay, but also by the precariousness of his position"[103]. This quotation is unfortunately an appropriate description of what is still happening in some developing countries. Entry into the public service is often secured by (financially) supporting a political party during its election campaign. These investments are supposed to be paid back via a political or civil servants position, including the condoning of corrupt practices by the prevailing political culture.

Baumol's central hypothesis is that the set of rules and *not* the supply of entrepreneurs or the nature of their objectives, undergo significant changes from one period to another and helps to dictate the ultimate effect on the economy via the *allocation* of entrepreneurial resources, which can better benefit from what the market mechanism has to offer.

The implication of Baumol's point of view is that – in cases where necessary – an adjustment in the rules of the game would help to introduce a more conducive allocation of entrepreneurial resources. Baumol investigated a few long-range historical processes (i.e., ancient Rome, medieval China, dark age Europe, the later Middle Ages) and found that the rules of the game do change dramatically from one time to another, and also, that entrepreneurial behavior changes direction from one economy to another in a manner that corresponds to the variations in the rules of the game. After all, the prevailing laws and legal procedures of an economy are prime determinants of the profitability of activities such as rent-seeking.

Baumol concludes that we do not have to wait patiently for slow cultural change in order to find measures to redirect the flow of entrepreneurial activity toward more productive goals. It may be possible to change the rules in ways that help to offset undesired institutional influences or that supplement other influences that are taken to work in beneficial directions. The success of putting these measures into effective practice depends on the question of how much the measures impinge upon the ability and willingness of the polity as well as the legal system.

Overall conclusion

It may be useful to treat government as an *integral* element of the economic system, functioning sometimes as a substitute and other times as a complement to other societal actors. In this view, government policy is not only aimed at introducing a substitute mechanism for resolving market failures, but also at creating an environment that promotes the capabilities of the private sector. And, regarding its public function (i.e., the part that cannot be performed by the market), it aims at executing this function effectively, supported by a meritocratic, efficient and transparent public service.

References

Balazs, E., 1965: *Chinese Civilization and Bureaucracy: Variations on a Theme* (New Haven: Yale University Press)

Bauer, P., 1987: *Equality, the Third World and Economic Delusion* (London: Weidenfeld & Nicolson)

Baumol, W., 1990: *Entrepreneurship: Productive, Unproductive, and Destructive* (Journal of Political Economy; Volume 98, number 5)

Castañeda, J., 2003: *The Forgotten Relationship, Rethinking US-Latin American Ties* (Foreign Affairs, May/June)

Fairbank, J., and Reischauer, E., 1984: *China, Transition and Transformation* (Sydney: Allen & Unwin)

Finley, M., 1965: *Technical Innovation and Economic Progress in the Ancient World* (Econ. History Review, August)

Grindle, M., 1996: *Challenging the State* (Cambridge: Cambridge University Press)

Lal, D., 2000: *The Poverty of Development Economics* (Cambridge MA: The MIT Press)

Oakeshott, M., 1975: *On Human Conduct* (Oxford: Clarendon Press)

Oakeshott, M., 1993: *Morality and Politics in Modern Europe* (New Haven: Yale University Press)

Plato, 1987: *The Republic* (Hammondsworth: Penguin Classics)

Popper, K., 1977: *The Open Society and its Enemies* (London: Routledge)

Sen, A., 1999: *Development as Freedom* (New York: Anchor Books)

Smith, A., 1937: *The Wealth of Nations* (New York: Modern Library)

Stiglitz, J., 1989: *The Economic Role of the State* (Oxford: Basil Blackwell)

Streeten, P., 1995: *Thinking about Development* (Cambridge: Cambridge University Press)

The Economist, 1997: *Survey on The Future of the State* (September)

Wolf, M., 2001: *Will the Nation-State Survive* Globalization? (Foreign Affairs, January/February)

Annex I

Since the French Revolution, six phases in the evolution of the global economy can be identified after the mercantilist system broke down because of its internal contradictions[104].

The *first* was the great liberal international economic order (LIEO) created under British leadership after the repeal of the Corn Laws in 1846. The next 20 years were the heyday of worldwide free trade. This period also saw the development of the intellectual justification for this order in Ricardo's famous law of comparative advantage.

With the rise of protectionism in the US and Germany in the 1860s and 1870s, new arguments for protectionism also arose associated with the names of Hamilton and Friedrich List. This *second* period of creeping protectionism, and the scramble for empire, culminated in the First World War. It was during these first two phases that much of the Third World was integrated into the world's economy, and many of them began their own process of modern economic growth, which has been identified as a sustained rise in *per capita* income.

The *third* period from 1913 to 1950, encompassing the two world wars and the Great Depression, can be looked upon as one during which the 19th century international trading and payment system, which had transmitted the growth impulse around the world, broke down.

It led in turn to the inward-looking policies most of the Third World adopted in the *fourth* of our periods, which spans the end of the Second World War and the first oil price shock of 1973. During this post-war Golden Age ... except for a few small countries on the Pacific Rim, most developing countries did not emulate the developed countries, which gradually liberalized the controls on foreign trade and payments they had instituted during the inter-war period.

But the example of the New Industrialized Countries, the disappointing results of their past dirigisme, and the process of dealing the multiple shocks in the volatile global economy ushered in by the OPEC coup in the 1970s, led in the *fifth* period (covering the 1970s and much of the 1980s) to an intermittent but gradual movement away in most of the Third World from "inward" to "outward" looking policies.

This marks the beginning of the latest *(sixth)* period. The collapse of the Second World in 1989 accentuated this trend towards liberalization. The global economy has at last taken off from where it broke down – first slowly and then cataclysmically in the course of the late 19th and the first half of the 20th century.

Annex II

Plato's thinking on the design and functioning of a state was inspired by his teacher Socrates (who, as you know, did not write anything) and on the experiences gained with various forms of democracy that Athens had known during Plato's lifetime[105]. At the time, *all* voting members of society had a say in Athens' government, as the Greeks never invented representative government. The sovereign body was the *Assembly*, a mass meeting of all adult male population (slaves and women had no voting rights).

The Assembly took all political decisions. As it was not practical to meet regularly, a *Council of Five Hundred* was formed to: carry on business of state between meetings; take care of routine and financial business; and draft business for future meetings of the Assembly. This Council was further subdivided into *Committees of Fifty*, each of which was responsible for carrying on public business for one-tenth of a year. The Council never became a continuing body with a policy of its own; the Assembly remained supreme. Such a complete system of popular control had never been known before or since. And it is important to remember that this, and not any form of modern *representative* government, was the background to Plato's comments on democracy, which basically involved *government by perpetual plebiscite*.

Given the above context, it is not so surprising that Plato's criticism of the people at large was that in many political matters they were bad judges. The common man has no experience or expert knowledge of such things as foreign policy or economics, said Plato, and to expect any sensible judgment from him on such matters was to expect the impossible. This drawback may be overcome by good leadership. But, here comes Plato's second criticism: democracy encourages bad leadership. People's judgment of their leaders is not always good, and they cannot be trusted to make the best choice. The popular leader, dependent as he is on his position of popular favor, will constantly be tempted to retain that favor by the easiest possible means. Popular leaders are as devoid of true knowledge as are the people they lead. Plato continues by saying that the salient characteristic of democracy is liberty: every individual is free to do as he likes. There was, according to Plato, a growing dislike of authority, whether political or moral. Where there is so little social cohesion, dissension follows inevitably. Politically, it takes the form of a struggle between the rich and poor finally degenerating in a class war. The poor have no use for the rich except to squeeze taxes out of them; the rich retaliate, and the freedom which the democrat claims will be a freedom of *two nations*, the rich and the poor, to fight it out among themselves as to who shall have the larger slice of the cake.

In summary: democratic government is weak and it is liable to degenerate into a bitter class struggle between the haves and have-nots. Finally, in tyranny, we see the danger that the violent and criminal instincts, normally kept under control, will get out of hand. Disunity, incompetence and violence, which he had seen in Athens and at Syracuse, were the main dangers against which Plato thought society must be protected.

What he proposed instead was how society, or the state, should be organized. The *Republic* deals less with questions such as: how is the state's sovereignty to be executed; what should the relations be between the legislature, executive and judiciary; and how is executive power to be administered? Plato was more interested in principles than in details. *The Republic* was written in the years after Plato's founding of the *Academy*, whose aim was to train philosopher statesmen, while the *Republic*, a statement of that aim, was bound to deal with education. Plato decided that the world's ills would not be cured till philosophers ruled; the education of philosophers, therefore, was to be the most important of political activities.

Education

Plato accorded a very high importance to education. He founded the *Academy*, which was the first university in Europe. He also had an eye for what we nowadays call primary and secondary education. The academic education was not to put knowledge into the mind that was not there before but to "turn the mind's eye to the light so that it can see for itself. In other words, the pupils should learn to think for themselves. As for the provision of education, this must exclusively be provided by the state. Anything of such importance cannot be left to private initiative. And because of its crucial importance in forming the minds – and character – of the young, the curriculum must be controlled and defined by the state".

Society and politics

Under this heading appropriately comes what Plato said about the (i) class system, (ii) property and the family, and (iii) the philosopher ruler. The class system, he said, was based on occupations, and not on income-groups. Plato applied his class distinction also to the army and government. Plato's Guardians were not only the professional soldiers, but also the government officials, subdivided into Rulers and Auxiliaries, roughly corresponding to Government and Army-Executive-Police, as opposed to the rest of the population, who together made up the third class. He does not tell us a great deal about this third class. They were not in any sense a proletariat or working class. They comprised all those engaged in economic activities – farmers, manufacturers, traders, you name it. All were allowed to own property. Their function was to provide for the material and economic needs of the community. Their virtue was obedience, and it is pretty clear that they would have been under strict control.

The function of the Rulers was to govern, that is, to take all necessary decisions of policy, which is the business of government to take. The Auxiliaries' function was to assist the Rulers in the execution of their decisions. We can think of them as combining the functions of civil service, military, and police. And if we think of a society in which there is a government by full-time, trained experts, who are precluded by law from any other function, and who have a body of trained civil servants, together with the necessary police and military forces, we get some idea – in modern terms – of this part of Plato's proposals. To rise in the system, the incumbent must pass many promotion bars; the highest grade is reserved for the Rulers. The third class had no say in matters of government; but Plato constantly emphasizes that the Rulers had their interests at heart and governed with the willing consent of the governed, says Plato. Yet, the third class could enter into the higher class, and demotion from higher to third class was possible as well. What Plato wanted to create with this was an aristocracy of talent. He thought that this could be created by breeding, implying by education and by arranged sexual intercourse – via marriage festivals, where suitable partners would be mated – so as to expect the best possible outcomes. This sounds a bit like Aldous Huxley's *Brave New World*.

Part of this unorthodox view may have been inspired by Plato's desire for equality between the sexes. He wanted to free women from child rearing by creating state nurseries, which would hand over that role, so as to free women from that obligation and allow them to pursue their proper career. Moreover, Plato assumed that family connections (such as a marriage) may only be a source of weakness: that the good family man must be a worse citizen.

As for the philosopher ruler, this is the central theme of *The Republic*. In it Plato says that the aim of the educational curriculum was to produce him! At the end of a long course of training there was left a small class of those who survived all tests, up to the age of 35(!); they were the Philosopher Rulers. They represented the highest talent, were given the highest training and were put at the disposal of the state. They did not serve the state because they wanted to; they were philosophers who had seen the supreme vision and preferred to spend their time in philosophy. But they had a duty to their fellow men, and they discharged this by doing the work of government, which fitted their training; they were a dedicated minority ruling in the interests of all.

Comments

Plato's thinking is weak on the implications of power. The ruling class has all the power and the third class has none. Plato's system, in other words, is not that it trusts the common man too little but it trusts his rulers too much. Among his critics, Karl Popper was the most formidable[106]. A résumé of his criticism follows below. It is important to note that Popper wrote his criticism in the early 1940s, during the time of his exile in New Zealand, having fled the tyrannical rule of the Third Reich. As Plato had little sympathy for democracy as practiced during his time, Popper had little sympathy for Hitler's national socialism and Stalin's communism! Plato, according to Popper, was a totalitarian who was opposed to all liberal or humanitarian ideas. He said that Plato was a *Utopian*, in the sense that his approach to political problems was to prepare in advance a blueprint of the society at which he aimed and then ruthlessly put it into effect. He similarly supposed that politics could be reduced to an exact science. Plato was a planner, and had an approach more characteristic of the Virtuous Left. The Soviet Union was perhaps the state most closely run on Platonic principles.

Popper maintained that Plato, in his desire to restore unity and harmony after the disastrous failure of Athens democracy, identified the "root of the evil" as being the "Fall of Man". Tyranny was not the solution, the end must be a complete return to nature, in other words to a closed society. As Popper stated: "He transfigured his hatred of individual initiative, and his wish to arrest all change, into a love of justice and temperance, of a heavenly state in which everybody is satisfied and happy and in which the crudity of money grabbing is replaced by laws of generosity and friendship. This dream of unity and beauty and perfection, this aestheticism and holism and collectivism, is the product as well as the symptom of the lost group spirit of tribalism" (p.199). Popper ended his criticism by stating: "For those who have eaten of the tree of knowledge, paradise is lost. The more we try to return to the heroic age of tribalism, the more surely do we arrive at the Inquisition, at the Secret Police, and at romanticized gangsterism" (p. 200).

110

The Institutional Dimension of Economic Growth

History matters.
Douglass C. North, *Preface to Institutions, Institutional Change and Economic Performance* (1990)

The first challenge in the development of whatever society is economic.
Kishore Mahbubani, *Can Asians Think?* (1998)

The causes of the richness and poverty of nations is the grand theme of all inquiries in Political Economy.
Malthus to Ricardo, Letter of 26 January 1817

Whatever is formed for long duration arrives slowly to its maturity.
Samuel Johnson, *The Rambler* (1750-1752)

Introduction

What are the determinants of economic growth? That is the theme of this essay. At the beginning of the 20th century there were scholars who thought they had found the answer. Take Ellsworth Huntington, for example. In his book *Civilization and Climate* of 1915, the influence of climate is an important determinant of the lagging behind of tropical countries. Huntington observed that most people lived in the open air, which led to a devaluation of moral standards so much so, to put it in his own words: "That their thoughts and energy are largely swallowed up in matters of sex". This prevented them from engaging in more economically productive activities, said Huntington[107].

111

Which factors explain growth or stagnation, and why is economic growth in the world's history the exception and not the rule[108]? Thinking a bit deeper about these questions, one realizes that economic science alone will most probably not be able to provide the answer. Other sciences – such as history and political science – may have to be called in. Or, perhaps, there is no universal answer or conceivable theoretical model that may explain economic growth. The economic historian Douglass North said the following about this dilemma: "... we are simply deluding ourselves if we believe that a single scientific explanation of the past is possible, but we are selling the discipline of economic history short by not trying to work toward that goal"[109].

This is really the most fundamental challenge for development economists and for those involved in development cooperation. Poverty – and thus the failure of economic growth – is the most pressing issue on the international agenda. Poverty is a threat to world peace and to the sustainable use of scarce resources. Poverty is an affront to civilization. For the billions of poor women, men and children, to be poor is a tragedy. Economic growth is a vital prerequisite for the eradication of poverty.

Broadening the perspective

Traditional economic growth models, in which the savings and investment rate, technological and managerial advancement, as well as population growth play vital explanatory parts, have recently been broadened by the inclusion of the *nature-nurture* dichotomy: would climatic, ecological and geographical conditions be crucial in explaining economic growth, or rather, would the institutions and culture play decisive parts in the explanation? The latter refer to the way an economy is organized, the way in which property rights are being applied, and how the relation between science and technology evolves.

Exceptional thinkers

Fortunately for us a few formidable thinkers have published some influential books over the recent past. I already mentioned Nobel laureate Douglass North, who is a prominent representative of the New Institutional Economics (NIE) school of thought. His book *Institutions, Institutional Change and Economic Performance* (1990) is innovative and is quoted by many scholars. The physiologist and ecologist Jared Diamond's *Guns, Germs, and Steel* (1997), provides a "short history of everybody for the last 13,000 years", as its subtitle says. In 1998, the historian David Landes published his masterpiece entitled *The Wealth and Poverty of Nations*, in which he explains why some societies are so rich and most others so poor.

Hernando de Soto is yet another contemporary author whose latest contribution to the debate on growth and development is called *The Mystery of Capital* (2000), in which he emphasizes the importance of the recognition of property rights for the development of the (in some countries) huge, informal sector.

What these authors propose can be found reflected in analytical studies and in policy papers of influential development institutions, such as the World Bank's: *Beyond the Washington Consensus; Time for Institutional Reform*[110].

What will be dealt with?

North's thinking will be dealt with in what follows and the question of whether or not a universal theory on economic growth can be expected. Furthermore, the results of a recent study in the domain of NIE will be presented, after which the question about convergence between rich and poor countries will be touched upon. This essay concludes with a brief treatment of the *nature-nurture* views on development.

Neo-classical growth theory

To explain why North is really an innovator, it is necessary to summarize the basics of the neo-classical growth theory, since North refutes some of its assumptions while he builds on others. In doing so he tries to bridge the gap between theory and the real world, thus bringing us one step closer to the universal explanation of economic growth.

Neo-classical economics applies the theory of rational expectations. This assumes that "agents" (i.e., decision-makers) form expectations based upon all available information about the future at the time they take decisions. So, agents only make random errors in foreseeing the future course of market variables. Since markets always clear, and since agents do not make systematic errors, full employment equilibrium is the economy's normal state of affairs. Prices will always adjust (i.e., *getting the prices right*) to ensure that there are neither unsatisfied buyers nor unsatisfied sellers in any market, including the labor market. The neo-classical theory, reflects a mathematical precision and elegance, and models a frictionless and static – but unrealistic – world.

The neo-classical theory assumes that in the face of pervasive scarcity, individuals make choices reflecting a set of desires, wants, or preferences. These choices are made in the context of foregone opportunities. Thus the opportunity cost of working an additional hour (and receiving additional income), for instance, is leisure foregone. This *rational choice* postulate assumes that individuals have a stable set of preferences for income, leisure, and so forth, and that the choice made at the margin (that is when an individual decides to work an additional hour) represents a trade-off between what one gets (more income) and what one must forego (leisure). This behavioral postulate operates in any kind of economic system: capitalist or socialist.

North's critique

North questions the neo-classical theory because it is portrayed in a world that seems frictionless, in which institutions do not exist, and all change occurs through perfectly functioning markets. In such a situation, the costs of acquiring information and transaction costs do not exist! The neo-classical theory is concerned with the functioning of markets, and not how markets develop over time. It does not explain persistence for millennia of what would appear to be inefficient forms of exchange.

North asks how policies can be prescribed when it is not understood how economies develop? When applied to economic history and development, the neo-classical theory focused on technological development and – more recently – on human capital development, but ignored the *incentive structure* embodied in institutions that determined the extent of societal investment in those factors. Hence, the neo-classical analysis of economic performance through time contained two erroneous assumptions that: (i) neither institutions mattered, (ii) nor did time.

North's body of thinking

The beauty of North's contribution to the theory of economic growth is that he refuted some of the assumptions of the neo-classical theory, whilst maintaining the scarcity and competition dimension. He added the vital role played by institutions, based on his insights into historical processes of economic growth and stagnation. In 1993 he received the Nobel Prize for Economics for his contribution to economic science.

North states that institutions are the main underlying determinant of sustained economic growth of countries. He defines institutions as the humanly defined *constraints* that structure human interaction. These constraints can be formal constraints (such as laws, rules, constitution) and informal ones (such as norms and conventions), and their enforcement characteristics. Together, they define the *incentive structure* of societies, and specifically of economies.

Rules of the game

A large part of *Institutions, Institutional Change and Economic Performance* explains how institutional change occurs. It is the interaction between institutions and organizations that shapes the institutional evolution of an economy. Institutions define *the rules of the game*, whereas the organizations and their managers are the players. Organizations in North's understanding are groups of individuals bound by some common purpose to achieve objectives.

Path dependence

Change may be of a revolutionary nature; however, as a rule change is an incremental process. Hence – according to North – institutions typically evolve in a gradual manner. The gradual and piecemeal natures of change processes follow a certain path. Understanding the structure of the institutional framework, and therefore a clear understanding of the implications of choices we make today for the functioning of the economy tomorrow, can only be gained by studying the actual history of development.

Transaction costs

Institutions – and the technology employed – determine the transaction and transformation costs that add up to the production costs. When it is costly to transact, then institutions matter. And it *is* costly to transact! North and Wallis calculated that more than 45 percent of the GNP of the US in 1970 consisted of transaction costs, such as banking, insurance, finance, wholesale; or in terms of occupations: costs of lawyers, accountants, and the like.[111]. This percentage had increased from approximately 25 percent a century earlier. Transaction costs are costs of specifying what is being exchanged and of enforcing the terms of contracts. In economic markets the attributes of the value of goods and services

116

are being specified, not only in their physical aspects but also in the form of property rights. However, it is the *polity* that defines and enforces property rights and, consequently it is not surprising that efficient economic markets are so exceptional.

North has given up his earlier optimism regarding the emergence of efficient property rights over time. *Institutions, Institutional Change and Economic Performance* are, amongst others, aimed at explaining how inefficient property rights can persist. North finds the answer in the inefficiency of political markets, arguing that both high transaction costs and errors in the perceptions of participants in political markets can produce property rights that do not induce economic growth. These property rights can, more-over, result in the creation of new organizations, designed to prosper under existing laws, which consequently have no incentive to create more efficient economic rules. Private gain is then made at the cost of overall economic growth. This is exactly the situation in many developing countries.

All these favor activities that promote redistributive rather than productive activities. They create monopolies rather than competitive conditions, and they restrict opportunities rather than expand them. They seldom induce investment in education that increases productivity. The organizations that develop in this type of institutional framework will become more efficient, yet more efficient at making the society even more unproductive and the basic institutional structure even less conducive to productive activity.

Such a path can persist because the transaction costs of the political and economic markets of these economies – together with the subjective models of the actors – do not lead them to move incrementally toward more efficient outcomes. This explains why these economies remain stagnant.

For all these reasons institutions are not necessarily or even usually created to be socially efficient; rather they, or at least the formal rules, are created to serve the interests of those with sufficient bargaining power to influence the creation of new rules. On the other hand, if economies realize the gains from trade by creating relatively efficient institutions, it is because under certain circumstances the private objective of those with the bargaining strength to alter institutions, produce institutional solutions that evolve into socially and economically efficient ones. North notes that the capture by organizations of the gains from trade for all parties to a transaction requires the development of the state as a coercive force, able to monitor property rights and the enforcement of contracts. However, the inability of most societies to develop effective, low-cost enforcement of contracts is, according to North, the most important source of both historical stagnation and contemporary underdevelopment in the Third World.

Quite a few developing countries provide good examples of anti-development frameworks that frustrate rather than promote growth: statist regulation, ill-defined property rights, failing enforcement of contracts, and so forth. These conditions result in rent-seeking and redistribution, not growth and rising productivity.

North believes that the key to sustained economic growth is a flexible institutional matrix that will adjust to technological and demographic changes. Successful political/economic systems have evolved such characteristics over long periods of time. The critical issue is *how* to create such systems in the short run, or – indeed – whether it is even possible to create them in short periods of time. North doubts if the policies that will produce an efficient allocation are always the proper medicine for ailing economies. These policies that are perceived to be inequitable will engender political reactions, which can stall or reverse effective reforms.

A critical evaluation

North's introduction of transaction costs and the demonstration of their significance is a major contribution to our understanding of development, and likely to be of enduring significance to the social sciences. This understanding has helped to nuance a few unrealistic assumptions of the neo-classical growth theory, thereby creating new research challenges and it has brought a shift in the way we think about development.

However, the problem with the institutional dimension of economic growth is that it has been mainly applied in descriptive historical studies. What Deepak Lal, the development economist, said about this is that there is no hope of incorporating institutional development in economic growth theory[112]. Other critics state that North's point on the fundamental role of institutions in the development process should be empirically checked. Moreover, proving that one institution is more efficient than another is conceptually more difficult than North's account might suggest since favorable economic outcomes, for example, do not necessarily imply that an existing institutional structure was better than possible alternatives.

Some critics, such as Robert Bates, state that it would be necessary to embed the NIE in the study of politics, as the structure of political institutions affects which economic institutions are chosen. Though it is correct that the choice of institution depends on the structure of transaction costs, it is the state that determines the *allocation* of these costs. In Bates' own words: "Once politicians are seen as determining the magnitude and distribution of these transaction costs, then a different vocabulary becomes relevant: that of political science"[113].

A grand theory or no grand theory; that's the question

Does North provide us with the universal theory on economic growth? The answer is: no, not yet. Nevertheless, I believe that his contribution is a firm step in that direction. North himself points out that we still know all too little about the dynamics of institutional change and particularly the interplay between economic and political markets. Unfortunately, research in the new political economy has so far largely been focused on developed countries. A great deal is known about the characteristics of the *polities* of Third World countries, whereas there is very little *theory* about such policies. Furthermore, demographic theory and its historical implications for the re-evaluation of past economic performance have yet to be integrated with institutional analysis.

The same applies to technological change. Recent insights produced by Joel Mokyr[114], exploring the impetus for and consequences of technological change have ongoing implications that need to be integrated with institutional analysis. Whatever the shortcomings, I believe that North belongs to that league of thinkers who developed *grand theories* such as Adam Smith, Karl Marx, and Arnold Toynbee[115].

What's new?

The reason why the New Institutional Economics is labeled New is because – as so often – others have pointed to the importance of institutions, way before North and others did. For example, in the *Wealth of Nations* Adam Smith argued that the British colonies of North America had a physical endowment poorer than the colonies of Spain and Portugal and no better than those of France, but explained their superior economic growth by noting that: "The political institutions of the English colonies have been more favorable to the improvement and cultivation of this land than those of any of the other three nations"[116].

Later on, institutionalism flourished in the US. Thinkers, such as the eccentric economist Thorstein Veblen pointed to the dichotomy between business and industry on the one hand and institutional and technical aspects on the other. This would help explain societal and organizational constraints on, or reactions to, innovation and diffusion of new technology. The Old Institutional Economics maintained that economic systems evolved as a result of adjustments to existing institutions, provoked by technological change.

Recent research

In response to the call for empirical studies, Knack and Keefer measured the impact of the institutional environment on the development of Third World countries[117]. They suggest that deficient institutions underlie the falling back of poor countries (contrary to the neo-classical belief of "catching up"), compared to the growth of developed countries. They employ various indicators of institutional quality, including the Rule of Law, the pervasiveness of corruption and the risk of appropriation and contract repudiation. Their results indicate that in the absence of good institutions, *convergence* slows. This manifestation of the "the poor are getting poorer" appears to be a direct consequence of the low quality of the institutions in poor countries.

Inadequate institutions degrade the security of property rights. Institutions that protect these rights include independent judiciaries, a division of executive and legislative powers that provides checks and balances, well-defined administrative procedures, and transparent decision-making. These institutions also inhibit governments from making dramatic or frequent policy change.

When property rights or the policy are not credible, firms are likely to make less efficient adjustments to technological change or to government policies[118]. Poor institutions that cannot guarantee the protection of property rights can also interfere with growth by promoting entrepreneurs who are less able to take advantage of new technologies. Where institutions are inadequate, entrepreneurs succeed on the basis of political rather than economic criteria; inefficient entrepreneurs survive who happen to have personal ties with state officials who are necessary to protect against expropriation, according to Knack & Keefer (K&K). If technological progress in a particular industry is limited by the ability of the most able entrepreneurs, then growth suffers when non-economic characteristics determine which entrepreneurs survive.

K&K admit the methodological difficulties in measuring the influence of institutions. For example, they state that the relative contribution of different institutions to the protection of property and contractual rights is not yet well understood. They illustrate this as follows: "Singapore, the United States and France all seem to possess little risk, relative to most countries, of expropriation or contract default, yet they achieve this result with markedly different institutional structures. The independence of the judiciaries in them varies considerably, as do electoral and legislative constraints on the executive branch and the nature of hiring and promotion processes in administrative agencies. It is not yet clear how these various institutional traits ought to be weighed in designing an objective measure of institutional quality"[119].

Another difficulty, according to K&K, is that rule obedience is likely to vary across countries, which would create biases in measures of observed institutional quality[120]. Their overall conclusion is that human capital acquisition, machinery and foreign investment, as well as foreign trade are all suggested as main vehicles for international transmission and absorption of technology. The one explanation for insufficient levels of any of these, however, may be poor institutions. If this is the case, breakdowns in foreign investment or human capital accumulations should be considered as proximate but not fundamental to the causes of low growth rates and the failure to catch up.

A recent publication: *Political Institutions and Economic Growth in Latin America*[121] provides more empirical evidence of the relevance of institutions for growth. It contains essays in which the discipline of the new historical economics, the NIE, and the new political economy have being applied so as to better understand why Latin America is lagging behind in its economic development. An important conclusion drawn by Douglass North and Barry Weingast is the following: "What is striking about Latin America... is how political decisions in Latin America so frequently bias the rules away from those that produce efficient markets. Explaining this political bias, in our view, will dominate the literature in the years to come"[122].

Convergence

Convergence between poor and rich countries is an important assumption of the neo-classical growth theory: the lower the starting level of real per capita gross domestic product (GDP) in relation to its long-term (or steady state) position, the higher the predicted growth rate. This results from diminishing returns to capital. Poor countries would grow faster than rich ones, as each slice of new investment gives higher returns in poorer countries.

Economies that have less capital per worker, therefore, tend to have higher rates of return and higher growth rates. However, if economies differ in various respects – including propensities to save and have children, willingness to work, access to technology, and government policies – then, the convergence force applies only in a *conditional* sense. For example, a poor country that also has a low long-term position (possibly its public policies are harmful, or its saving rate is low) would not tend to grow rapidly. Robert Barro confirmed this *conditional convergence*, through a study in which he compared the performance from 1960 to 1990 of 100 countries[123].

The big question is whether convergence between rich and poor countries will eventually take place. Rapid growth of the four Asian Tigers and other South and East Asian countries during the past four decades does raise hopes. Moreover, the pace of economic development of successful growers accelerated in the course of time. For example, it took Great Britain, 58 years (from 1780), the United States 47 years (from 1839), and Japan 33 years (from 1880) to double their economic output. More impressive still is Indonesia, which took 17 years, South Korea 11 years, and China who managed to double its production in only one decade!

Mancur Olson provides a rather *down to earth* observation regarding convergence[124]. Simply put, he argues that if countries are wasting resources, they can achieve a spectacular rate of growth by using their available resources better. Olson presents evidence that labor, capital, and knowledge are being massively squandered in many poor countries. He says that the economic potential of poor countries is enormous, as demonstrated by the Asian Tigers. His explanation, coinciding with that of Barro, is that poor countries can converge if they were to exploit their respective economic potential. The reason this potential is often not tapped is that, according to Olson, the incentive structure in many poor countries is counterproductive and the institutional framework is inadequate. Olson concludes that the quality of economic policies and that of institutions explain the difference between poor and rich countries.

Regarding actual convergence, Olson notes that the fastest growing countries are never the ones with the highest per capita incomes, but always a subset of the lower-income countries. During the 1970s, for example, South Korea grew seven times as fast as the United States. In the same period, the four countries with the highest growth rates per capita (i.e,. Botswana, Malta, Singapore, and South Korea) grew on average 6.9 percentage points faster per year than the United States[125].

North is less optimistic about convergence, taking into consideration ten millennia of development and stagnation. An overwhelming feature of the last ten millennia is that we have evolved into radically different religious, ethnic, cultural, political and economic societies. North also observes that the gap between rich and poor nations is wider than ever before.

As for the large difference in wealth between North America and Latin America, he says: "In the former, an institutional framework has evolved that permits the complex impersonal exchange necessary to political stability and to capture the potential economic gains of modern technology. In the latter, personal relationships are still key to much of the political and economic exchange. They are consequences of an evolving institutional framework that produces neither political stability nor consistent realization of the potential of modern technology"[126].

Nature or nurture

Jared Diamond wrote a prize-winning book entitled *Guns, Germs and Steel*, describing in lucid and engaging style humankind's history spanning a period of 13,000 years. Diamond summarizes his message as follows: "History followed different courses for different peoples because of differences among peoples' environments, not because of biological differences among people themselves"[127]. The big difference between Diamond and other authors of grand theories before him is that the latter skipped the early formative ages of human history by paying little or no attention to prehistory and non-literate societies.

Eurasia availed of a variety of favorable circumstances that promoted sedentary agriculture, which in turn allowed for specialization and the formation of states. Eurasia forms a very large territory, whose "axis" stretches from West to East, and thus provides similar climatic conditions for promoting the relative rapid spread of agricultural practices and related technological inventions throughout the region. Comparing this with Africa and the America's, their axis runs vertically from North to South, thus encompassing varying climatic conditions (including tropical ones), which limit the spread of crops that thrive in cooler climates. Moreover, the spread of agricultural practices was greatly hampered by barring deserts in both continents and, for the America's, the extreme narrowness of Central America.

On top of all this, when the Europeans came to the America's, they brought with them germs to which they were resistant, but not the indigenous American populations. The latter were consequently almost wiped out by killer diseases, but also by the brutal slaughter which accompanied colonization. The conquest by Francisco Pizarro of Inca emperor Atahuallpa, on the 16th of November 1532, was an example. It was also symbolic, according to Diamond: "Thus, Atahuallpa's capture interests us specifically as marking the decisive moment in the greatest collision in modern history. But it is also of more general interest, because the factors that resulted in

Pizarro's seizing Atahuallpa were essentially the same ones that determined the outcome of many similar collisions between colonizers and native peoples elsewhere in the modern world. Hence, Atahuallpa's capture offers us a broad window onto world history"[128].

Nurture

Let us now look at the nurture dimension. In this respect, the historian David Landes is a formidable representative. In his book *The Wealth and Poverty of Nations*[129], he explains growth or stagnation as a result of cultural factors rather than climatic or geographical ones, though they are not entirely excluded.

The point is, according to Landes, *how* societies deal with adverse conditions. If we learn anything from the history of economic development – says Landes – it is that *culture* makes all the difference. He illustrates this with the extensive treatment of the Western/European cultures wherein curiosity, the freedom of thought and expression, entrepreneurial capacity, the desire to prosper, trust, diligence, and initiative are being promoted. "Until very recently, over the thousand and more years of this process that most people look upon as progress, the key factor – the driving force – has been Western civilization and its dissemination: the knowledge, the techniques, the political and social ideologies, for better or worse. This dissemination flows partly from Western domination, for knowledge and know-how equal power; partly from Western teaching; and partly from emulation. Diffusion has been uneven, and much Western example has been rejected by people who see it as an aggression"[130].

However, the question is how to integrate the relevance of culture into a development model that in turn would offer the universal explanation of growth, but also of stagnation. In response, let me end with a final quotation of what North said about the role of culture: "Informal constraints matter. We need to know much more about culturally derived norms of behavior and how they interact with formal rules to get better answers to such issues. We are just beginning the serious study of institutions. The promise is there. We may never have definite answers to all our questions. But we can do better"[131].

Conclusion

I do not believe that the opinions of Diamond and Landes are contradictory; they are *complementary*. The advantages that Europe had at the time, climatically and geographically speaking, helped to develop its cultural traits and, thereafter its discovery and domination of the rest of the world.

I believe that nurture, namely, the political and institutional setting of societies, nowadays plays a more dominant role in understanding economic growth – or the lack of it – than nature does. Douglass North provided us with an analytical framework, and he indicated which elements were still missing in completely explaining growth or stagnation. His contribution has meanwhile been included in the application of various disciplines. Whether we will get closer to the full understanding of the determinants of economic growth will now depend on the progress to be made in these disciplines.

Update

Since I wrote this essay in 2001, research on the influence of institutions on the process of change and development has progressed. As Douglass North noted, we already knew the economic and the institutional conditions that make for good economic development. What we did not know, according to North, was how to get them[132]. The central question in development is what exactly triggers economic growth? The impact of the NIE led us to believe that it is institutions that do the trick.

However, an important recent article nuances this insight. The article is entitled: *Do Institutions Cause Growth?*[133]. What the authors say, based on historical and empirical evidence, is that it is human capital accumulation that triggers growth, which *in turn* leads to institutional improvement. The article presents basic econometric regressions, as well as a variety of additional evidence that suggests that: (i) human capital is a more basic source of growth than institutions; (ii) poor countries get out of poverty through good policies; and (iii) they subsequently improve their political institutions.

Seymour Martin Lipset, a representative of the development view whose thoughts were inspired on Aristotle's, provides the intellectual basis for this insight[134]. Lipset believed that educated people are more likely to resolve their differences through negotiation and voting than through violent disputes. Education is needed for courts to operate and to empower citizens to engage with government institutions. Literacy encourages, amongst others, the spread of knowledge about government's malfeasance. According to this view countries differ in their stocks of human and social capital, which can be acquired through policies pursued even by dictators. Institutional outcomes largely depend on these endowments. What is not dealt with by the authors, however, is how to explain the difference in stocks of human and social capital. I fear that one would then have to enter the slippery domain of culture – slippery, because it might lead to politically incorrect conclusions.

The institutional and the development view coincide with the emphasis that both put on the need for *secure property rights* to support investment in human and physical capital, and they both see this security as a public policy choice. However, the institutional view sees pro-investment policies as a consequence of political constraints on government, whereas the development view sees these policies in poor countries largely as choices of their often autocratic leaders.

The article's authors refer to the respective growth experience of South Korea, Taiwan, and China, which grew rapidly under one-party dictatorships; the first two eventually turning to democracy. Another example would be Chile´s *take-off* under Pinochet.

The comparison between North and South Korea is illustrative of the authors' message. Prior to the Korean War, the two countries were obviously part of one, so it is difficult to think of them as having different histories. They were both exceptionally poor in 1950 and both were dictatorships between the end of the Korean War and 1980. If institutions are measured by Polity's "constraints on the executive", which is probably the best of measures commonly used in the literature, then North Korea had an average score of 1.71 and South Korea 2.16 (out of 7) between 1950 and 1980. Yet, South Korean dictators chose capitalism and secure property rights and the country grew rapidly, reaching a per capita income level of USD 1,589 in 1980. The North Korean dictator, in contrast, chose socialism, and the country only reached the level of income of USD 768 in 1980. Starting in 1980, South Korea transformed itself into a democracy, while North Korea remained a dictatorship. While *on average*, looking over the half century between 1950 and 2000, South Korea obviously had better institutions as measured by constraints on the executive, these institutions are the outcome of economic growth after 1950 rather than its cause. It would be wrong to attribute South Korea's growth to these institutions rather than its choice made by its dictators[135].

Each community faces a set of institutional opportunities, determined largely by the human and social capital of its population. The greater the human and social capital the more attractive its institutional opportunities. And institutional outcomes also get better as the society grows richer, because institutional opportunities improve.

The authors of *Do Institutions Cause Growth?* conclude that the initial level of human capital of a country and the average level of its institutions over a period of time predict its level of economic growth, whilst past educational investments continue to be strong predictors. As for sequence, the authors demonstrate that economic growth and human capital accumulation *cause* institutional improvement, rather than the other way around.

As historical and empirical evidence supports this insight, the article of Glaeser et al. has highly relevant implications for policy-makers in poor countries and for the donor community, in that poor countries may need to emphasize the promotion of economic growth through human and physical capital development and through ensuring property rights. Economic growth in these countries may be feasible without immediate institutional improvement, but will ultimately lead to it.

References

Barro, R., 1996: *Determinants of Economic Growth: An Empirical Study of Various Countries* (Cambridge, MA: Harvard University Press)

Bates, R., 1995: *Social Dilemmas and Rational Individuals* In: Harriss, J., Hunter, J., and Lewis, C., *The New Institutional Economics and the Development of the Third World* (London: Routledge)

Burki, S., Perry, G., 1998: *Beyond the Washington Consensus: Time for Institutional Reform* (Washington: World Bank)

De Soto, H., 2000: *The Mystery of Capital* (New York: Basic Books)

Diamond, J., 1997: *Arms, Germs and Steel: A Short History of Everybody for the Last 13,000 Years* (London: Vintage Books)

Glaeser, E., La Porta, R., Lopez-de-Salines, F., Shleifer, A., 2004: *Do Institutions Cause Growth?* (Cambridge, MA: National Bureau of Economic Research Working Paper Series)

Haber, S., et.al., 2000: *Political Economy and Economic Growth in Latin America* (Stanford: Hoover Institution Press)

Keefer, P., Knack, S., 1997: *Why don't Poor Countries Catch Up? A Cross-National Test of an Institutional Explanation* (Economic Enquire, Vol. XXXXV)

Lal, D., 2000: *Institutional Development and Economic Growth* In: Oosterbaan, M., De Ruyter van Steveninck, T. and Van der Windt, N., *The Determinants of Economic Growth* (Boston: Kluwer Academic Publishers)

Landes, D., 1998: *The Wealth and Poverty of Nations: Why Some are so Rich and Others are so Poor* (New York: Norton)

Lipset, S., 1960: *Political Man: The Social Basis of Modern Politics* (New York: Doubleday)

Mahbubani, K., 1998: *Can Asians Think?* (Singapore: Times Books)

Mokyr, J., 1990: *The Handle of Richess* (New York: Oxford University Press)

North, D., 1981: *Structure and Change in Economic History* (New York: Norton)

North, D., 1990: *Institutions, Institutional Change and Economic Performance* (New York: Norton)

North, D., 2001: *Needed: A Theory of Change* In: Meier, G., Stiglitz, J., *Frontiers of Development Economics: The Future in Perspective* (Washington: Oxford University Press)

Olson, M., 1996: *Big Bills left on the Sidewalk: Why Some Nations are Rich and Others Poor* (Journal of Economic Perspectives, 10 (2))

Smith, A., 1937: *The Wealth of Nations* (New York: Modern Library)

Wallis, J., North, D., 1986: *Measuring the Transaction Sector in the American Economy* In: Engerman, S., Gallman, R.: *Long-Term Factors in the Growth of the American Economy* (Chicago: Chicago University Press)

The Evolution of Development Economics

A study of the history of the opinion is a necessary preliminary to the emancipation of the mind.
John Maynard Keynes, *The End of Laissez-Faire.*

Development economists are both effects and causes: effects of the politics and institutions of their time; causes (if they are fortunate) of beliefs which mould the politics and institutions of later ages.
Bertrand Russell, paraphrase of Russell's statement in: *A History of Western Society.*

Introduction

Is economics difficult or not? The famous economist John Maynard Keynes once had dinner with the equally famous physicist Max Planck, the inventor of quantum mechanics. Planck told Keynes that he once considered going into economics himself. But that he decided against it as the subject was too hard for him! Keynes repeated this story with relish to a friend in Cambridge. "That is odd", said the friend, "Bertrand Russell was telling just the other day that he had also thought about going into economics. But that he decided it was too easy".

In this essay the evolution of development economics forms the central topic. The difficulty with development economics is not so much that it is complicated but that it has difficulty in explaining *what exactly* triggers development. The central question is whether economic science can provide a *universal* explanation about economic growth or not. Important strides towards that universal explanation have been made, in particular, new economic institutionalists such as Douglass North contributed greatly. They highlighted the important role played by institutions in explaining economic growth. However, in my essay on the *Institutional Dimension of Economic Growth*[136], I concluded that economics alone cannot explain development. Other social sciences, such as anthropology and political economy, have to be called in to help provide the answer.

Evolution of development economics

The World Bank took the excellent initiative to publish a book entitled *Frontiers of Development Economics*, which includes contributions from 33 development thinkers and an agenda for future research. I will deal with some of their contributions, putting them in a historical perspective[137].

It is not a coincidence that the subject of development economics evolved after the end of the Second World War. It was at that time that the second wave of decolonization also emerged. Asian and African colonies obtained political independence from former colonizers such as Britain, France and the Netherlands. To achieve *economic* independence, however, the newly independent governments had to seek advice from economists from, especially, the United States and England. This promoted the emergence of development economics as a separate domain of economics in the early 1950s[138].

Gerald Meier, who wrote the introductory chapter to *Frontiers of Development Economics*, distinguishes a *first and second* generation of development economists[139], as follows below.

The first generation

Let us start with the first generation. They led the thinking from 1950 to roughly 1975, and formulated grand models of development strategies that involved structural transformation and an extensive government involvement in the development process. Because the population was rapidly growing, the emphasis had to be on a rapid rate of growth of the production function: the gross domestic product (GDP). Capital accumulation was the central focus of the model. There was a residual factor as well, helping to fully explain total factor productivity. This consisted of a coefficient of (exogenous) technical progress.

The Harrod-Domar equation, although originally formulated for conditions of full growth in an industrial economy, was (erroneously) applied to estimate capital requirements in developing countries[140]. Other early models of development strategy also featured capital accumulation, such as Rostow's well-known "stages of economic growth", Nurkse's "balanced growth", and Rosensein-Rodan's "external economies" and "big push". These models require strong state action. In the belief that a developing country did not have a reliable market price system, that the supply of entrepreneurship was limited and that large structural changes were needed, the first generation of development advisers turned to the state as the major agent of change[141]. With these macro-strategies it was believed that government could accomplish a structural transformation in the developing economy. Government would give reality to Rostow's "take-off", would promote Rosenstein-Rodan's "big push", and would break Nurkse's "vicious circle of poverty".

Above all, the first generation of development economists was full of optimism, reflective of the optimistic spirit of the post Second World War epoch, radiating the message that bridging the gap between rich and poor countries could be done! Capital infusions to promote investments (and technical assistance to make it work) were the main instruments of early development aid. It was just a matter of time, it was thought. True enough, there was pessimism about developing countries' capacity to export primary products and to pursue export-led growth.

Critique

In the early 1970s, especially after the first oil crisis of 1973, these grand models were criticized for their lack of empirical evidence. Experience with the adverse effects of ineffective and incompetent government interventions that undermined free market forces, shattered the belief in the first generation's development prescriptions[142]. Moreover, unemployment was not decreasing, the numbers of people living in absolute poverty increased, and the gap between the *haves and have-nots* widened.

In the 1970s critics pointed to the causes of government failure: unsustainable intervention in the market, institutional weakness, inadequate information and resources as well as failings in the delivery of public goods and services. Although the rationale for government interventions had been to remedy *market failure*, the perverse result was only too often *government failure*, and this was increasingly evident in price distortions and the resulting slump.

Getting the prices right

The policy challenge became "get the prices right". Although a necessary condition for development, it certainly was not a sufficient one. However, "getting the prices wrong" frequently meant the end of development and the beginning of crisis, as we had seen in the early 1980s in many Latin American and African countries.

Second generation

The first generation of development economists was visionary; the second can be characterized as realistic, grounded on fundamental principles of *neo-classical economics*. Governments were admonished to remove price distortions and thus to get all prices right. Not differences in initial conditions, but differences in *policies* were now thought to explain the disparate performances of developing countries. A country was not poor because of the vicious circle of poverty, but because of poor policies.

The neo-classical philosophy dismissed the earlier claim that development economics had to be a special sub-discipline in its own right. The neo-classicists maintained that the postulates of rationality and the principles of maximization had universal applicability. In accordance with neo-classical economic theory, whose focus is on microeconomics, the second generation of development economists moved from the first generation's highly aggregative models to disaggregated micro-studies in which the units of analysis were production units and households.

Whilst in earlier concepts of the aggregate production function the residual was thought of as a coefficient of technical advance, the second generation's perception of the residual was seen to be as a composite of the effects of many different forces such as: (i) improvement in the quality of labor through education; (ii) reallocation of resources from low-productivity uses to higher ones; (iii) exploitation of economies of scale; and (iv) improved ways of combining resources to produce goods and services.

The Asian Miracle

In the 1980s, the East Asian Tigers became *the* success story of development. Inspired by their phenomenal economic growth, it was felt that the correct policies were to move from inward-looking strategies toward liberalization of the foreign trade regime and export promotion, so as to introduce stabilization programs, privatize state-owned companies and to follow the dictates of the market price system. Through its guidance toward correct policies, neo-classical economics was believed to be the safeguard against policy induced distortions and non-market failures[143].

New endogenous growth theory

The first generation's emphasis on physical capital formation did not bring the expected results. More weight was now given to human capital, to create agents who could become more productive through their acquisition of knowledge as a source of *increasing returns.*

By emphasizing knowledge and ideas, the new endogenous growth theory of the 1980s brought about a marked change in the analysis of the aggregate production function. Instead of the early neoclassical Solow version of diminishing marginal returns to physical capital, the new growth theory examines production functions that show increasing returns, due to an expanding stock of human capital, and to specialization and investment in knowledge capital, because knowledge can be used repeatedly at no additional cost.

The role of ideas and knowledge

A great many ideas, inspired by the available stock of knowledge and by the spirit at the time, contributed to development, realizing that aid alone could not yield development. As for ideas, Paul Romer said that: "Ideas should be our central concern... Ideas are extremely important economic goods, far more important than the objects emphasized in most economic models. In a world with physical limits, it is discoveries of big ideas, together with the discovery of millions of little ideas that make persistent economic growth possible. Ideas are the instructions that let us combine limited physical resources in arrangements that are more valuable"[144].

The ultimate objective for appropriate ideas should be absorbed and implemented in developing countries. These ideas include both concepts of development policy, in a macro sense, and ideas about technical progress, in a micro- or enterprise sense. Beyond contributing to technical change and raising the growth rate, the absorption of ideas may also facilitate the structural transformation of the economy, allow better control of demographic changes and improve the distribution of income. In an even deeper sense, scientific ideas and rationality can change a society's values and can give support to modernization.

Ideas are transferred not only through international trade, foreign direct investment and technology. It can be argued that international cooperation has also a very prominent role to play in the transfer of successful development ideas that can benefit recipient countries. Former World Bank Chief Economist, Joseph Stiglitz, noted that the World Bank has shifted much of its emphasis to the intangibles of knowledge, institutions and culture in an attempt to forge a more Comprehensive Development Framework. The Internet will no doubt also help in bridging the knowledge gap, provided that the users know *how* to spot the appropriate ideas and transform them into effective development actions, supported by a favorable political and institutional environment.

For developing countries, this new *endogenous* growth theory has thus meant a greater emphasis on human capital (including learning), even more than on physical capital and recognition of the benefits from the international exchange of ideas that accompanies an open economy integrated into the world economy.

Convergence

The new growth theory is also relevant to the question of *convergence*. This occurs when the technology gap between countries is overcome and poor countries catch up with rich ones by simply growing faster. Free mobility of capital among countries will speed this convergence as the rate of diffusion of knowledge increases, so it was thought.

The *catching up* idea is for the time being restricted to a few successful so-called emerging economies, resulting in an increasing heterogeneity between developing countries. This begs the question *why* certain development policies are effective in a few countries only, and not in others.

New political economy

The inquiry into the causes of differential development perform-ance led to more attention to the *politics* of policy-making. The first generation of development thinkers looked upon the state as an exogenous force. The new political economy attempts to *endogenize* the decisions of politicians and bureaucrats having, amongst others, given rise to an over-extended and exploitative state.

Market failures

A major modification of the neo-classical analysis occurred in the mid 1980s when new market failures were analyzed by Douglass North and others. The recognition of the existence of imperfect and costly information, incomplete markets, increasing transaction costs, and so forth, led to the emergence of the *new institutional economics*.

State of the art

These new insights triggered a consensus in the 1990s, namely the promotion of policy reform. The state was believed to be over-extended. A market price system was needed to get the prices right. And to also get the policies right, there was a need for stabilization, liberalization, deregulation and privatization. In other words, the *Washington Consensus* was born! But, to get the prices right *and* to get the policies right, it is also necessary to get the *institutions* right! As North observes, we know a good deal about what makes for success-ful development, but we still know very little about *how* to get there and, especially, how to establish the institutional framework that will support the desired rate and composition of economic change.

This is where we stand today. Yet, there are still many unanswered questions to be dealt with by the next, third, generation of devel-opment economists. Gerald Meier proposed a few fundamental ones, some of which will be briefly dealt with in the next section.

Patterns of growth and income distribution

For the older generation the main question was how to promote economic growth, i.e., the increase in per capita income. However, nowadays we are not only concerned with *growth* but also with *development*, which is growth plus change, including issues such as better income distribution, equal opportunities for men and women, the protection of the environment and, as Armatya Sen pointed out, development as *freedom*[145].

If poverty is to be reduced, future analysis will have to pay more attention to how the pattern of growth determines who are its beneficiaries. The creation of jobs will obviously help fight poverty. This is the more pressing, as the world's labor force will increase by 40 percent in the next twenty years, with 95 percent of the increase in developing countries, where less than 15 percent of the world's capital investment will occur[146]. To reduce poverty by increasing productivity and earnings, governments will have to devise appropriate policies in four crucial sectors of the economy: (i) the rural sector; (ii) the urban informal sector; (iii) the export sector; and (iv) the social sector.

Understanding the sources of growth

Another challenge for future development economists is the composition of the residual factor in the aggregate production function. In the first generation this residual factor was technological progress. However, there are many more aspects that probably form part of the residual factor. Growth accounting still has to establish the *interactions* in the residual among technological progress, economies of scale and scope, human capital, knowledge capital, and institutional change. Furthermore, the economies of ideas and knowledge require extension. Questions will have to be answered such as: if deliberate technological progress is to be achieved, what is the institutional design that will motivate behavior for the creation of knowledge?

The influence of institutions

As for institutional change, Douglass North already said that we still don't know how to promote the process of economic development, in particular how to establish the institutional and organizational structure that will support the desired rate and composition of economic change. In a developing economy, it is especially important that institutions both facilitate and adapt to change. To do this, a country must be capable of much social invention so as to provide *incentives* to people to cooperate in economic activities.

Social capital

The term *social capital* is in vogue. It succeeds "human capital" and "knowledge capital" as a new determinant of growth. But, what is meant by social capital? Paul Collier defines it as: "The internal social and cultural coherence of society, the norms and values that govern interactions between people and the institutions in which they are embedded"[147]. But, is the appeal to social capital anything more than an appeal to consider culture and institutions? And if this were so – which I believe it is – this would move the explanation of the process of change into a multidisciplinary endeavor.

Globalization

More than for previous generations, open economy models will be the rule in the foreseeable future. Whereas previous international policy issues revolved around trade policy, the next generation of development thinkers will have to devote more attention to diminishing the negative effects of globalization because there is a growing concern that globalization may not benefit some developing countries and their poor populations. In this respect, Meier observes that: "WTO, IMF and the World Bank will have to devise new programs to ensure that the benefits of global integration are more equally shared, that competitive policymaking is avoided, and that problems of incomplete risk markets are mitigated as international integration becomes ever more complex"[148].

The role of the state and the market

The role of the state and that of the market in reducing poverty and promoting economic growth will be the dominant theme in future development economics. The future will probably move away from the *minimalist state* concept. Instead, a *capable state* will have to face the new market failures; it will have to effectively and equitably provide education and health. It has a vital role to play in improving income distribution. It must uphold human rights, and provide roads and bridges; it has to protect the natural environment.

It would be useful to treat government as an integral element of the economic system, functioning sometimes as a substitute for, and at other times as a complement to, other societal actors. In this view, government policy is not only aimed at introducing a substitute mechanism for resolving market failures, but also at creating an environment that promotes the capabilities of the private sector. And, regarding its public function (i.e., that part which cannot be performed by the market), execute this function effectively, supported by a meritocratic and efficient public service.

A blending of public policies with the market will involve much deeper conceptual issues than those that faced the managers of command economies. In many ways it will be more difficult to be policymaker, policy-adviser and policy-administrator all at the same time.

Policymaking

Crucial to policy reform is an understanding of the reasons for the success of government policy. The new political economy ignores *critical moments*, namely, turning points such as a change of government or a crisis situation, when policy changes can occur. Deepak Lal says, for example: "... a 'crisis' provides an opportunity for liberalizers – but it may be of short duration. A big bang may therefore be desirable to smash the equilibrium of rent-seeking interest groups who have a stake in maintaining the past system of dirigisme. To stiffen the government's spine in the unenviable task, sweeteners which ease its fiscal problems in the form of soft loans or grants from multilateral and bilateral foreign governments, may be desirable"[149].

In situations like these, economists tend to have less understanding of the policymaking process. The problem is not so much technical but, rather, highly political and entails political and social change. The political process of economic policymaking matters in these circumstances, which one still finds in quite a few poor developing countries.

To promote policy reform, economic and political advisors will have to examine feasible ways of: compensating the losers; discovering the possibilities for building supportive coalitions; and considering the scope for alternative institutional arrangements. It will be especially important to insulate policymakers from rent-seekers and interest groups, so that the government can give more attention to the growth of the economy and less to distribution of favor-seeking groups.

Rationale for development economics

As long as developing countries have characteristics that distinguish them from industrial countries, a sub-discipline of development economics will be relevant. Even though there is a set of basic economic principles, their particular application in any country will depend on the economic structure, institutions, political regime, administrative capacity, culture and history of the particular country.

Conclusion

Initially, growth accounting emphasized capital accumulation. The simple Solow decomposition of growth into factor contributions, and a residual, was based on a differentiation of the production function: $Y=F(K,L,t)$, where Y is output, K is capital, L is labor, and t is time. The residual – that is to say growth in total factor productivity – was left to be explained exogenously by technical progress. Notions about growth were based on conventional growth theories. The assumptions about the institutional quality and capacity of the main societal actors (especially Government) and their interplay were projected onto developing countries. Practice showed, however, that this was wrong. Indeed, many developing countries did not take-off. Worse still, many stagnated; the divide between the haves and have-nots widened. Only a few exceptions – amongst them the Asian Tigers – did show that growth could be achieved.

Supported by research of other disciplines, second generation development economists discovered that developing countries offered a distinctly different cultural, political, institutional and technological environment. Moreover, the notion of economic growth has given way to a wider, more qualitative, term: economic development, involving income distribution, respect for human rights and environmental protection. The first generation residual factor of exogenous technical progress in growth accounting, therefore, had to be amplified by endogenous factors such as culture, politics, institutions, social capital, and so forth. This implies that development economics alone cannot explain let alone predict economic growth and development[150].

When looking back on what the evolution of development economics has taught us, we see that development analysis has to start with understanding and mapping the culture and belief systems of distinct developing societies. Together they mould the *polity*, that is the way in which politics is being conducted. And it is politics that decides on the scope and form of institutions. Institutions encompass the *rules of the game* of a society, which in turn explains whether economies are growing or stagnating. Thus, development economics cannot do without other disciplines that help understand the cultural and political dynamics of developing societies. It is in this soil that economic seeds are sown. Ultimately, whether or not the seeds will grow and flourish depends on the fertility of that soil.

References

Ackley, G., 1961: *Macroeconomic Theory* (New York: Collier-Macmillan)

Collier, P., 1998: *Social Capital and Poverty* (Washington: World Bank Social Capital Initiative Working Paper 4)

Lal, D., 2000: *The Poverty of Development Economics* (Cambridge MA: The MIT Press)

Lewis, A. 1952: *The Principles of Economic Planning* (London: Allen & Unwin)

Lewis, A., 1955: *The Theory of Economic Growth* (London: Allen & Unwin)

Lewis, A., 1969: *Some Aspects of Economic Development* (Accra: Ghana Publishing Corporation for University of Ghana)

Meier, G., Stiglitz, J., 2001: *The Frontiers of Development Economics: The Future in Perspective* (Washington: Oxford University Press)

Romer, P., 1993: *Idea Gaps and Object Gaps in Economic Development* (Journal of Monetary Economics, 32, December)

Samuelson, P., 1970: *Economics* (New York: McGraw-Hill)

Sen, A., 1999: *Development as Freedom* (New York: Anchor Books)

Summers, L., 1991: *Research Challenges for Development Economics* (Finance and Development, 28, September)

Part II

Articles

Nine recipes for successful economic development

Bolivia is poor and will stay poor if it does not improve its economic health. Bolivia's past economic performance demonstrates little success: stagnation was the rule, bouts of insufficient economic growth the exception. What could be done to change this and to embark on a path toward sustained economic growth? I humbly propose nine recipes, inspired by what successful economic growers tell us, and my appreciation of Bolivia's bottlenecks.

1. Invest in the technical and intellectual capacities of the people
It is the people themselves who are achieving development. The better equipped they are the greater the chance of success, therefore, ensure that everyone has access to education and make education more efficient. Educate the students which the private sector needs, especially in technical and technological fields. Improve the quality of academic education. Bolivia has 40 private universities in addition to several public ones. This *oversupply* erodes the quality of academic teaching. Limiting the number of universities and introducing much stricter entry criteria would be the way forward.

2. Weed out red tape and enforce property rights
Do away with unnecessary and costly requirements to register business firms. Pointless regulations only foster graft and corruption. The World Bank recently calculated that while it takes 203 days to register a firm in Haiti, this is done in only 4 hours in New York. The city of La Paz dramatically did away with red tape – an example that should be copied rapidly in the entire country.

Moreover, any investor, whether foreign or local, will think twice before putting money into an enterprise if his property rights are not well protected.

3. Exploit Bolivia's economic comparative advantages

Apart from its gas reserves, Bolivia avails of a few nearly monopolistic comparative advantages: quinua, llamas, tourism – to name a few – all of which have not been exploited to date. The government should vigorously promote private investors to do so. All products are labor intensive so it would create not only income but also employment. True, Bolivia has huge gas reserves, but it would be unwise to only count on them for its development, because the proceeds may be inadequate to finance Bolivia's development needs. Moreover, this may create a perverse element in public finances, as the Dutch know better than anybody else. The Dutch Disease was characterized at the time by a misbalance of public finances, high inflation and deteriorating competitiveness of Dutch export products.

4. Forge regional economic integration and favorable trade agreements

Bolivia's internal market is small and has limited purchasing power; hence its expansion is in the interest of Bolivia's producers. Its competitiveness, moreover, is in urgent need of improvement (Bolivia ranks 3rd lowest in the World Economic Forum's Business Competitiveness Ranking!). It is then that economies of scale could be achieved. The European integration is an example to follow. Trade agreements with the US, Japan, and the EU should be continued and deepened.

5. Make the public sector more efficient

Salaries of civil servants increase annually like, for example, salaries of university personnel that have risen by 7% annually over the past five years. Did these rises translate into better academic education? No. The public sector needs to be improved and made more transparent. Hiring and firing of staff should be done on the basis of their merits and performance. And, the public sector should be managed and rewarded on results achieved.

6. Fight corruption

This is easier said than done, as large parts of Bolivia's society and culture are infested with corruption. Corruption is like a cancer that spreads throughout the body. Where to start? Simplifying bureaucratic procedures helps. The same applies to well-equipped and properly paid investigators of corruption plus an independent judiciary. Changing cultural patterns is a matter for the long run through introducing ethics into school curricula, and so forth. The fight will be a long and hard one.

7. Make development aid more effective

The other day a Bolivian colleague asked me how much had the donor community invested in Bolivia since democracy was restored in 1982. I figured that it could have been around USD 8 billion. He then – suggestively – asked what the effect of this huge amount (equivalent to Bolivia's GDP) was. Sure enough, the assistance helped in financing the road network and other infrastructure, and in investing heavily in education and health. Bolivia had also received large amounts of budget support. Despite all of this the number of poor increased by 200,000 during the last decade. The share of the private sector in the national economy dropped to 12 percent and Bolivia is still the poorest country in South America. But, aid alone cannot develop a country; international investment would be a great help, and – above all – Bolivia's own performance is crucial. Nevertheless, aid givers should channel their support much more toward the direct promotion of economic growth, including the creation of an attractive environment for private (and informal) sector development.

8. Value entrepreneurship, discipline and perfection

These are other cultural aspects. Recipe 3 mentioned the untapped resources that Bolivia can exploit. Why has that not been done? A lack of entrepreneurship forms part of the explanation. Without dynamic people who are prepared to take risks and work long hours, Bolivia's richness cannot be exploited to the full. Discipline and striving hard to produce quality products and services are other indispensable ingredients for success. Both elements are in my appreciation still lacking in Bolivia's culture.

9.   Don't lose hope; it can be done

Bolivia has a lot going for it. It is a matter of getting things done. Other developing countries have proved that it can be done. Compare Bolivia with South Korea, for instance. In the 1950s both countries were equally poor. South Korea has applied all the recipes I described above. It now boasts of an average per capita income many times higher than Bolivia's!

An economic think tank for Bolivia

I have the curious – but fairly useless – habit of trying to find out where things come from, so, the other day I lifted up my coffee cup at *Alexander Coffee* to see where it came from. Underneath it I read: Made in China. It seems as if almost all things nowadays are *Made in China*. The Chinese really do know how to benefit from globalization! Some view globalization as a threat: an evil invention of capitalists to dominate the world economy. I don't think globalization is a threat. On the contrary, it provides a marvelous array of economic opportunities. But does Bolivia grab these opportunities? I doubt it. True, Bolivian exports will reach a record high of USD 2 billion this year. But that is mainly the result of the – temporary – high prices of its minerals, soya and, indeed, its gas. Little processing of raw materials is being done in Bolivia, which as we know heightens their added value greatly. Bolivia has a few comparative advantages (i.e., quinua, llama's, alpaca, timber, tourism) which to date have not been exploited. Why is this? Bolivia is a landlocked country, its road network is inadequate and it has a small internal market. There are also *man made* limitations such as blockades and strikes that cost the Bolivian economy millions of dollars, worse still, they also shy away foreign investors.

Integrated growth policy

The challenge is: how can Bolivia's growth be sustained over time? Economic history demonstrates that it is sound government policies and private sector initiative that explain growth. Government designs an *integrated economic growth policy*, which provides the environment for entrepreneurs to produce, do business, and to

153

export. Europe, the United States, and – more recently during their *catch up* phase – the East Asian Tigers first applied infant industry promotion policies, so that they could mature. Moreover, all governments invested heavily in improving the spread and quality of education, especially in the technical and technological domain. Research was stimulated as well. Why was that? Because Governments understood that industry needed engineers and technicians to develop or adjust existing technology to specific circumstances. It is the level and quality of human capital – often preceding slow institutional change – combined with good economic policies that explain why economic growth can accelerate and be sustained.

More examples

In the nineteenth century the German government started a catching-up policy through its direct involvement in key industries and the introduction of advanced technologies from other countries, especially from Britain, which was well ahead of Germany at the time. Another intervention was the re-orientation of German teaching from law and theology to science and technology, which at the time were not even taught in Oxford and Cambridge! The fact that between 1820 and 1920 almost 10,000 Anglo Saxons went to Germany to study these subjects was proof of the quality of German higher education! Moreover, Germany pioneered modern social policy during the time of Chancellor von Bismarck, which was important to maintaining social peace and the creation of a healthy work force. Needless to say Germany overtook Great Britain in economic wealth within two generations!

The spectacular growth of the Asian Tigers is fundamentally due to activist industrial, trade and technology policies introduced by the state. Technology licensing and foreign direct investment were regulated in an attempt to maximize technology spillover. The countries skill base and technological capabilities were also upgraded through subsidies to education, training and R&D.

Think tank

The popularity of the Mesa Administration is based more on its handling of the political agenda than on its economic one. The latter seems not to be well spelled out. It is not *neo-liberal*; but then what is it? Buy Bolivian Products and the Hospital de Empresas form part of the policy, but what else? History shows that successful economic policies not only involve stimulating the private sector but also include strategic investments in education, research and social development. Such an integrated approach does not exist in Bolivia. This is serious and should be addressed soon. First, because the external environment for growth is favorable; second, poverty and unemployment need to be redressed so as to stop political instability; and third, Bolivia must finally step out of its *poverty trap*.

Export-led economic growth is the key to all this. Government can be helped in the design of an integrated economic growth policy through valuable inputs of a Think Tank composed of internationally renowned economists, like Bolivia's friends Joseph Stiglitz or Jeffrey Sachs. It would not be the first time that a developing country avails of such a think tank. Chile, Peru, Indonesia, Singapore, to name only a few, had them, and with success! Financing of this think tank should not be a problem; donors will certainly be interested in this proposal. The advice of this think tank can be fed into the already existing working groups between the Ministry of Economic Development and the employers. To effectively implement the strategy, a special *taskforce* could be installed composed of high-ranking officials with delegated authority from the Minister of Economic Development (if not of the President himself) to get things done. The taskforce would have the authority to take all bottlenecks away that stand in the way of rapid and effective implementation: *red tape* can be stripped, available funds can be tapped, the necessary coordination between Ministries be organized, and so forth. All this would put Bolivia on the road to sustained economic growth by exploiting its comparative advantages, thereby benefiting from the globalization process.

Will world poverty be halved by 2015?

I n 2000, world leaders gathered at the Millennium Summit in New York and committed themselves to halving poverty by 2015. A person is absolutely poor if he or she has to live of USD 1 per day. This objective raises three pertinent questions. First, why did donor and recipient countries alike agree on this objective, which incidentally is the first of the eight so-called Millennium Development Goals (MDGs)? Question number two is how can the achievement of this objective be measured? And third, can this MDG possibly be achieved, taking into consideration that around 2.7 billion people belong to the world's absolute poor?

Let us deal with question number one first: why did the international community agree on halving absolute poverty? The world of international cooperation can be characterized – over its half century of existence – as having applied successive development paradigms (i.e., filling the financing gap, big push, satisfying basic needs, good governance, etc.), which were supposed to help achieve development in Third World countries. Why this succession of paradigms? Because, thus far, none of them helped to effectively overcome the divide between rich and poor countries, whilst it is the developer's *raison d'etre* to achieve precisely that. New paradigms provide new challenges and fresh hopes to make headway. So far, public opinion in the donor countries bought all this. However, the financiers of development aid – namely, the taxpayers in the aid-giving countries – want to see results, hence, the emergence of the MDGs. These MDGs provide a measurable commitment to fight poverty. Yet, they beg for patience (i.e., up to 2015) to achieve them. Setting these goals is also *tricky*, because if they are not achieved *donor fatigue* may get the upper hand.

Whatever the paradigm, I believe what is really at stake is whether poverty worldwide can be eradicated to such an extent that *all* poor can live a minimally decent life. In this sense, it is important to distinguish different types of poverty. There is mass structural poverty, destitution and conjunctural poverty. China and India are well on the way to successfully fight mass structural poverty, thanks to their phenomenal growth rates during the past decade. However, destitution, i.e., the poor that are incapable of earning a living, can only be tackled if the State or charitable organizations provide help to them. And it will then depend on the level and quality of this welfare provided as to whether the destitute could be helped to lead a minimally decent life.

Statistics

Let us now turn to the question of whether the number of absolute poor can really be halved by 2015? This implies not only a tremendous development challenge but also a methodological one when it comes to measuring results. A lot of statistical effort is being invested in monitoring progress and, as always, there is no consensus on the statistical basis of measurement or on the reliability of the data. There are analysts who maintain that the objective of halving poverty has already been achieved, mainly thanks to China and India's growth, where 40 percent of the world population – including the bulk of the world's poor – live. The Washington-based Institute of International Economics (IIE) for instance, says that poverty has dropped decade by decade from 56 percent of the population of developing countries in 1950 to 9 percent in 2000. In fact, the IIE maintains that the first MDG had already been achieved when it was proclaimed in 2000. However, former chief economist of the IMF, Stanley Fischer, calculated growth in GDP per head proportional to population size. And here again, China and India stand out to the extent that on the basis of Fischer's calculation one must conclude that developing countries are catching up and world inequality is narrowing. Others disagree. It all depends on how poverty is measured. As for the methodological debate, there are two schools of thought. One takes National Accounts as the basis, such as the IIE, while the other takes household surveys as their basis, such as the World Bank. The UN uses their figures to monitor progress in the achievement of the MDG on the halving of poverty.

The outcomes of both differ quite a bit: based on National Accounts, the figures provide a rosier picture than the ones based on surveys. Why is this? The World Bank attempts to measure "consumption poverty", as opposed to "income poverty". If poor people still manage to save that means that their consumption will be less than their income; hence, there will be more people on the Bank's definition of poor people. Furthermore, the Bank expresses its poverty ratios as proportions of population in the developing countries, whilst National Accounts adepts use the entire world's population, with the result that the National Accounts-based estimates are smaller than the Bank's.

However, National Accounts fail to capture some aspects of non-market income and consumption. This makes them prone to *understating* the consumption of the poor, as well as overstating the growth of consumption of the poor, as income rises and as more activities fall within the scope of market transactions. Moreover, GDP taken from National Accounts includes much more than only household consumption. It includes, for example, also private investment and government spending. Hence, the estimates based on household surveys show more pessimistic trends in poverty.

Are the figures too pessimistic?

One can conclude that the official World Bank data, as used by the UN, are probably too pessimistic. Poverty has most likely fallen faster than the World Bank and UN figures suggest, and possibly fast enough to reduce the global headcount of those living on less than USD 1 per day, *even* as population rises.

The Economist recently invited Martin Ravillion of the World Bank's Development Research Group to comment on the discrepancies in the measures of poverty. He confirmed that the differences are directly related to the statistical bases used: National Accounts or household surveys. Though the levels differ substantially, both methods demonstrate the same trend: the global poverty rate almost halved. Ravillion also deals with the question as to why the Bank's figures are so much higher than those based on National Accounts. But are they really, Ravillion wonders? He brings to mind that National Accounts figures are based on GDP per head, and that GDP – as already mentioned – include much more than consumption of poor households. Hence, to make a justified comparison, the National Accounts' measurements should be heightened. However, the big question is by how much? That is hard to say. Ravillion proposed lifting the poverty line to USD 2 per day. If this criterion were to be applied to the National Accounts' figures, then the Bank's figures coincide with the former. The methodological ball is now in the court of National Accounts' adepts to confirm or refute Ravillion's conclusion that there is little difference in the *adjusted* outcome of both measurements.

Good news and bad news

The good news is that poverty has indeed fallen quite dramatically over the past two decades. But crossing the USD 1 or USD 2 borderline does not mean that all of sudden a person is no longer poor. A lot more income would be required to free the poor from their dismal position and to exchange it for a better, more decent life.

Another worrying fact is that the *absolute* number of people living on USD 2 a day has risen from 2.4 billion to 2.7 billion, a trend we also see in Bolivia. If we were to exclude the Chinese poor (who have graduated from the USD 1 per day borderline), then the number of poor has not changed much, whilst the *composition* of world poverty has changed noticeably: the number of poor in Asia has fallen, but risen elsewhere. It has roughly doubled in Africa. In the early 1980s, one in ten of the world's poorest lived in Africa; now the figure is about one in three. The figures for Bolivia are equally disturbing. Whereas the percentage of poor Bolivians declined during the past decade from 71 percent to 58.6 percent, their absolute number increased by 200,000 to 4.7 million. Thus, in Africa and in Bolivia, the fight against absolute poverty is far from being won.

Can the United States Win the War on Drugs in its Backyard?

The United States is a great country. It is the only superpower left and demonstrates imperial tendencies – perhaps against its own traditional foreign policy culture. On visiting the US one is immediately impressed by its pulsating rhythm of life. Everything there seems big and voluptuous, including – unfortunately – an increasing number of its inhabitants. It has the world's best universities, research institutes and newspapers. In short, there is much to be admired.

America's backyard

It is interesting to analyze the foreign policy of the US, as superpower, especially its relation with Latin America. My appreciation of it is a mixed one. The political influence in its Latino backyard is large, despite the fact that most Americans neither know nor care much about Latin America. There is little to boast of in terms of America's contribution to development and welfare. During the 1950s, American policy was heavily inspired by the then anti-communist mood. Latin American dictators were condoned as long as they withstood communism. A well-known *bon mot* regarding these dictators of the then Secretary of State, John Foster Dulles, is illustrative: "They are bastards, but they are our bastards!"

Free trade agreements exist with Latin America, NAFTA being one of them. Mexico is to benefit from it. Others, such as the Andean Free Trade Agreement (AFTA), are supposed to benefit Andean countries. However, I fear that America's good free trade intentions are undone by its counterproductive and destructive anti-drugs policy vis-à-vis Latin American coca growing countries. Although the anti-drugs policy is inspired by internal political considerations, its negative *spillover* in many Latin American countries adds to the United States' foreign policy headaches.

A long and costly war

President Nixon started the war on drugs some 30 year ago. To date, American taxpayers contributed USD 300 billion to this war that took many lives, greatly destabilized coca producing countries (such as Colombia), and promoted corruption and crime. And what was the result in the United States? Did it help fight cocaine and heroine addiction? The simple answer is: No! On the contrary, illegal drugs remain cheap and easily available throughout the States. Prices of cocaine have shown a downward trend, which is a reliable indication of a plentiful supply. All this may sound unbelievable, yet Ted Galen Carpenter's recent book *Bad Neighbor Policy* provides devastating evidence[151].

Galen first explains what the rationale was behind the effort to deal with the illegal drugs problem. This went as follows: taking into consideration that it would be difficult to dampen demand, if the supply of cocaine and heroine were to be shut off in the raw material producing countries of Latin America, then the price of cocaine and heroine would rise beyond affordable levels. Hence, the war on drugs had to be waged in the producing countries Colombia, Ecuador, Bolivia, Peru and, lately, Mexico. Coca eradication programs were introduced as early as the 1980s, when drug abuse became a top priority of America's foreign policy. Also crop substitution projects were introduced and drug trafficking was interdicted. The United States also offered more development and military aid. American military personnel became more and more involved in training their Latin American counterparts in surveillance activities to detect drug trafficking and production laboratories, thereby underlining that a true *war* was being waged. Countries that did not cooperate could count on economic sanctions, including an American vote against loans from the

World Bank and the Inter American Development Bank to offending countries.

Push down, pop up

Eradication of coca plants has proved not to work. When production is successfully pushed down in one region, fresh production pops up in another. Even the smashing of the Medallin and Cali cartels in the mid-1990s did not affect supply much. Galen notes that Colombian drug producers adjusted to the new environment and adopted a more decentralized form of business organization. Today some 300 loosely-connected families control the drug trade, and Colombia still accounts for approximately 80 percent of all the cocaine produced in the world and two-thirds of the heroin consumed in the US.

Crop substitution programs also do not work. The price of (illegal) coca production is simply much higher than any other crop. Galen states that the difference may be 4 to 10 times higher. Other estimates suggest that coca may even reach 50 times more! Another aspect in favor of coca growing is that it can be grown in remote regions with poor soil, places where alternative crops are economically not viable. Moreover, coca provides six harvests a year, whilst all others one or two at the most.

Coca growers do not have to bother about transportation and credit; this is catered for by drug traffickers who pay the farmers well and take care of transportation. In other words, crop substitution and eradication programs, as applied with the help of the US for more than a quarter of a century, simply ignore some of the *most basic principles of economics*. This is why they are inevitably doomed to fail! What the US is in fact asking from coca producing countries is to eliminate a significant portion of their economies, without adequate financial compensation. In Bolivia's case, Galen estimates that coca eradication did cost the economy between 13 and 15 percent of its GDP during the 1990s, whilst it provided the adult population with 20 percent of employment. The financial compensation received by way of uncompetitive crop substitution and alternative development programs was hopelessly inadequate. It should therefore surprise nobody that politicians like Evo Morales cash in on the – justified – hard feelings of the impoverished coca growers. In Colombia, left-wing guerilla organizations such as FARC are believed to earn between USD 500 million and USD 1 billion annually with the drug trade. At the time, the Maoist *Shining Path* in Peru also received funding from narco-traffickers. All this adds up to political instability, which is exactly what weak democracies, like Bolivia, cannot put up with as the persistent economic recession makes things only more difficult to handle.

What to do instead?

Mexico's ex-Foreign Minister, Jorge Castañeda hit the nail on the dot when he recently commented in Newsweek: "Indeed, the time is uniquely propitious for a wide-ranging debate between North and Latin Americans on this absurd war that no one really wants to wage. In the end, legalization of certain substances may be the only way to bring prices down, and doing so may be the only remedy to some of the worst aspects of the drug plague: violence, corruption and the collapse of the rule of law". The question is why was this useless war waged and for so long? What interests were at stake? At first, I thought that political and financial interests of the powers that be could provide the answer. But there is no evidence that US politicians would be implicated. True, quite a few Latin American politicians were involved, such as Panama's dictator Manuel Noriega and Peru's Secret Service chief Vladimiro Montesinos. A more convincing reason is provided by American public opinion. During the past 30 years, the war against drugs received majority approval of America's public opinion.

But there are now signs that this is changing. For instance, in a 2001 survey 74 percent of respondents did agree that the drug war was being lost. Equally revealing, only 6 percent considered illegal drug use to be the nation's most pressing problem, compared to 37 percent in a similar survey conducted in 1990. Hopefully, Arthur

Schlesinger may be right in his opinion that US interest in Latin America peaks and ebbs in 30-year cycles.

After 30 years of a lost war on drugs, the cycle should now go upwards via the only common sense approach to the problem: the legalization of certain substances, as Castañeda and many others already suggested. Why legalization and why certain substances? Legalization, because this would bring down the market price of drugs dramatically, and thus instantly take away the criminal and corruption dimension of the problem. Why certain substances only? Not all drugs can be legalized. Heroine, for instance, should not be legalized because it is highly addictive; a few doses are enough to turn a person into a junky. As with the highly successful anti-smoking campaigns, aggressive anti-hard drugs campaigns should go hand in hand with legalization. Addicts to cocaine should be put under medical control, so as to ensure proper, clean and regulated administration of the drug. Experiments in some European countries in this vein have shown positive results. What would all this mean for Latin America? The coca growers will be able to freely go on growing their traditional crop, but the market price will be lower. Crime, corruption and financing of political elements that intend to destabilize democracy, however, will diminish. All this will create a healthier environment in which democracies can be stabilized, economic growth can resume and the rule of law can prevail.

What ...If?

What would Bolivia look like if there were no foreign aid? Obviously it is only possible to speculate about the answer, as Bolivia has received billions of aid in dollars. Nevertheless, the question is intriguing and actual, as the international debate on the effectiveness of aid is again swinging in a negative direction. The basic question of this article can be divided into three sub-questions. First, if aid would indeed be ineffective, would developing countries then not be better off without aid? Second, does aid take away a *sense of urgency* in the acts of politicians in recipient countries? Third, does the *perverse* element in the relationship between recipient and donor not negatively affect the very objectives they say they share? It should be remembered that aid is only *one* instrument to promote growth and fight poverty. Foreign direct investment and the elimination of trade barriers are often more powerful instruments.

Aid effectiveness

Examples of how aid has not worked are well known. Just a reminder from Africa: Zambia's GDP per person was nearly twice South Korea's in 1964. By 1999, the Koreans were 27 times richer. Bolivia did not do much better than Zambia, despite billions of dollars of aid during the course of the past 25 years. Bolivia's GDP per head has not grown since 1973. What did grow was its number of poor: from 4.5 million in 1991 to 4.7 million in 2001, which is almost 60 percent of the total population. At best, aid may have prevented Bolivia from sinking deeper into trouble. True, aid has indeed played an important positive part in some fields.

The establishment of macroeconomic stability after the disastrous hyperinflation of the early 1980s comes to mind. Without the policy advice and financial help of the IMF, Bolivia would probably not have achieved this. And there is progress in the social sectors, especially health and education, promoted and co-financed by the donors. Access to health increased during the past decade from 46 to 62 percent. Illiteracy steadily decreased down to 13 percent in 2001, consequently schooling grades increased to 87 percent. Unfortunately, progress in the social sectors did not lead to economic growth; a worrying phenomenon Bolivia that shares with many other developing countries! Equally worrying is Bolivia's decreasing quality of academic education as a result of the large numbers of university entries and the mushrooming of private universities. Moreover, scientific research and technological improvement is scant and of poor quality.

The recent emphasis by donors on Good Governance may have its positive influence in the medium term on Bolivia's drive to modernize its public sector, to reform its judiciary, and to fight corruption. However, this process will find quite a few opponents in its path, who stand to lose their privileged economic and political position. Other aspects in which the donors played a positive role are attention for environmental and gender issues, but they are not yet very visible in Bolivia's policy *outcomes*. The same applies to the attention for poverty reduction: good intentions but no visible improvements.

What about private sector development?

There has been little attention from the donor community to promote the private sector, including the informal sector. This is strange, as the private sector is *the* sector that promotes growth. It is not so strange when one looks at the roots of the assistance philosophy. It says that to eradicate poverty and improve domestic income distribution, government intervention is required to redistribute assets and to manipulate the returns of different types of labor and capital through price and wage controls, so that scarce resources are used to meet the basic needs of the poor rather than the luxurious wants of the rich. Despite heavy investments by the donors in strengthening the state machinery in many developing countries, government of the typical Third World country has not performed well. There are only two highly successful examples of strong government performance in eradicating poverty: Pinochet's government and that of Lee Kuan Yew in Singapore. There is a growing recognition of the importance of the private sector – supported by the enforcement of property rights – in promoting growth. Obviously, aid funds cannot directly support the private sector, as it would influence the functioning of the free market. But aid funds can help in promoting an *enabling environment*, i.e., improving the *incentives* for the private sector to function efficiently and profitably.

Path dependence

Donors often project onto their recipients what they have achieved in their respective countries through the centuries, as something that can be repeated in a relatively short period in developing countries. But, history does matter. The institutions of the West developed gradually, while those of most new states were put into place in an elaborated form immediately. In the West, a civil society evolved side-by-side with the maturation of the modern state. This made possible the growth of representative institutions that confined the state's power to those matters that society was unable to deal with on its own. We donors, in our haste to see results, seem to forget that each recipient country has its own cultural heritage and its specific path along which development must take place. In other words, it is its history that moulds a country's destiny, and shortcuts to progress are possible only in exceptional cases as demonstrated by e.g., Singapore, South Korea, and Taiwan.

Sense of urgency

Does aid take away the sense of urgency in the minds and acts of politicians in recipient countries? Of course aid takes away at least *part* of this urgency. For example, if the aid did not foot half the bill of Bolivia's public investments year after year, the need to increase Government's proper income via customs and taxes would have been felt sooner and much more urgently. Now, between them, they only raise less than 10 percent of GDP, and worse still, this percentage is decreasing! There are several African countries with a lower income per capita than Bolivia's that nevertheless generate more income via their customs and taxes. Development is only possible if a country saves and invests, and its population pays adequate taxes to allow its government to provide public services for all. It is quite telling that the IMF and World Bank have to insist on a new Tax Law, and not Bolivia's Congress.

Then there is Bolivia's increasing budget deficit. At the moment this runs up to 8 percent; an unsustainable percentage. It is quite likely that without foreign aid, the government would have been forced to take measures to curb this deficit, e.g., by increasing taxes on petrol, and certainly not continue employing more public servants than it can afford. Without foreign assistance, it would probably be difficult to hide the fact that Bolivia is basically not a viable economic entity: 60 percent of its – small – population cannot generate effective demand as they are simply too poor. Hence, that demand is to be found beyond its frontiers. Expansion of its markets via economic integration with neighboring countries might have been higher on Bolivia's political agenda if they received no aid.

Perversity

The original idea of giving aid was that donor countries would support developing countries only temporarily – say, one generation – until they *took off*. Tanzania's late President Nyerere coined the term *self-reliance* for this perspective. However, the time horizon for taking off after which it could achieve sustained economic growth is dependent on the *path dependence* of a recipient country. Experience has shown that the graduation process from poor to a self-reliant country often takes much more time than one generation. Donors, however, are in a hurry. Aid ministers have to report successes to their parliaments and electorate. All this is probably why the ever-changing development fashions of the donors radiate renewed hopes for success. In many cases these fashions did not contribute to overcoming the specific hindrances to development of recipient countries.

Wishing to speed up the process, donors often introduced parallel structures to implement projects without looking at the need to strengthen the local capacity to take over those projects once donor support ends. Donors often fly in their own personnel or hire consultants whose salaries and perks are much higher than that of their local counterparts. Donors sometimes also create distortions in the recipient's labor markets. In Bolivia, for instance, the average civil servant's salary is 30 percent higher than in the private sector. This means that good people are lured away from the private sector to the public sector. Then, there is the multitude of varying procedures and requirements of every individual donor. Ministries in Bolivia are often supported by several donors, few of whom have the flexibility of putting their contributions in one basket, implying uniform procedures for all, thus freeing the recipient's limited capacity to attend to its core tasks. There are unfortunately still too many donors who simply lack the flexibility to enter into such arrangements. To my mind there is no reason why they could not harmonize their procedures. It would greatly help if the recipients, including Bolivia, would present programs for "basket funding" just to overcome this nuisance.

The way forward

The only real hope of eradicating poverty is to achieve sustained economic growth with effective redistributive policies. To achieve this in Bolivia takes two to tango. Bolivia's own policies so far brought about social but no economic progress. Poverty increased during the past decade. The donors, the other tango partner, apparently were unable to help turn poverty around, despite its prime objective to do so. Bolivia desperately needs more effective public policies to revert the situation and it needs to promote its private and informal sector. What the donors should do is not only overcome the perversities I just mentioned, but also follow a "no cure no pay" policy, meaning they should only finance development efforts that prove to be effective.

Two millenniums of economic development and how Latin America fared

In Angus Maddison's *The World Economy: a Millennial Perspective*[152], he presents an analysis of two millenniums of economic development. This is not, of course, the first book to take a long shot at development, but the first of its kind that supports the story with a systematic *quantification* of comparative economic performance. The book addresses questions such as: what factors explain growth or stagnation; what countries led the development process, and – the most pressing question at the moment – did *convergence* between rich and poor countries take place and, if not, what are the perspectives? Let us first look at the two millenniums of development in general, and then at Latin America's development in particular.

Over the past 1000 years the world's population grew 22-fold, per capita income increased 13-fold and the world's GDP nearly 300-fold. This contrasts sharply with the preceding millennium (from year 0 to 1000), when the world's population grew only a sixth, and there was no advance in per capita income; in other words it was a millennium of *stagnation*. In the course of time the leading countries/regions moved westwards: up to 1500 China led the way, benefiting from a market five times larger than that of Europe at the time, and from its superior shipbuilding techniques, compared to those of its competitors. After 1500, China was eclipsed by Western Europe (Venice, Flanders, the Netherlands and England, in that order). In the 19th century the US overtook England as the dominant economy in the world. From the beginning of the 20th century Japan and the Asian Tigers became the fastest growers. At this moment it is China, once again, which together with South Korea are the fastest growing countries.

Take-off

Maddison shows that world development really took off after 1820: per capita income rose more than eightfold and population more than fivefold. Of course, per capita income is not the only indicator of welfare. In the long run there has also been a dramatic increase in life expectancy: in the year 1000, the average infant was expected to live for about 24 years. Now, the average infant can expect to live to be 66.

Divergence

The growth process was uneven in space as well as time. The rise in life expectancy and income has been fastest in Western Europe, North America, Australia and Japan. The gap between this group of rich countries and the developing nations is widening. In 1820 the former had an income level twice that of the rest. By 1998 the gap was 7:1. However, when we look at the gap between the US and Africa it is now 20:1. Divergence instead of convergence is thus dominant. But, divergence is not unavoidable. The Asian Tigers have demonstrated during the past half-century that an important degree of *catching-up* is feasible. Moreover, the rapid growth of China and that of India (both with huge populations) resulted in a notable downward trend in the number of the world's poor.

Golden age

The golden age of economic growth was the period 1950-1973. The world economy grew then much faster than it had ever done before: world GDP rose by nearly 5 percent annually, and world trade by nearly 8 percent. The acceleration was greatest in Europe and Asia. There was also a degree of convergence between regions, though a good part of this was a narrowing of the gap between the US on the one hand, and Western Europe, Japan and the Asian Tigers on the other. If the world consisted only of these two groups, the pattern of world development could be interpreted as a clear demonstration of convergence. The Asian countries achieved a significant *catch-up* on the advanced European countries and the US, through success in mobilizing and allocating resources efficiently and improving human and physical capital to adapt to available technology.

Slow down

World economic growth slowed substantially after 1973, and the Asian growth was offset by stagnation elsewhere. The successive oil crises of 1973 and 1979 as well as the diminishing technological progress, explain this slow-down to a large extent. Moreover, the contribution of IT to productivity gains was too limited to offset the downward trend.

What factors explain development?

Maddison mentions three basic factors: (i) the conquest of relatively empty territories with fertile soils; (ii) international trade and capital movements; and (iii) technological and institutional innovation. The development of the Americas serves as a telling example of these factors. The major initial attractions of the Americas were the rich silver resources of Mexico and Bolivia, and development of plantation agriculture with imports of slave labor from Africa. The neo-European economies of North America and the southern cone of Latin America developed later. The indigenous population of the Americas did not – as we sadly know – recover its 1500 level until the first half of the 19th century. The full potential of the Americas began to be realized in that same century with massive European immigration and the western movement of the production frontier via the newly introduced railways.

Why North and Latin America differ

The present difference in economic performance between North and Latin America is partly the result of variations in resource endowment, but also because of strong institutional and societal echoes from the colonial past. In the former Spanish colonies the indigenous population remained as an underclass. Bolivia, unfortunately, is still *the* example in this respect. There were also important differences in the colonial period between the Iberian institutions and those of North America. These had a tremendous impact on subsequent growth performance. Maddison illustrates this by showing the difference between the United States and Mexico after they gained their independence in 1776 and 1825, respectively. The former showed a much greater dynamism than Mexico. How come? In Mexico a considerable part of domestic income went into the pockets of Spaniards who did not stay in the colony but took their savings back to Spain. The population of the British colonies in North America was better educated, had greater intellectual freedom and social mobility. In 1776, the 13 British colonies had nine universities for 2.5 million people, whereas Mexico had only two universities (in Mexico City and Guadalajara), for double the amount of people. Moreover, they concentrated on theology and law; subjects not the most appropriate ones to promote development. And during the colonial period the Inquisition kept a tight censorship and suppressed freethinking.

In Mexico *hacienda* owners engrossed the best land. By contrast, in North America the white population had much easier access to land; in New England family-farming enterprise was typical, supported by the enforcement of land property rights. Mexico was led by colonial rent-seekers, contributing little to Mexico's development. Finally, population growth in North America – as a result of the rapid inflow of migrants – was another source of advantage. Population in North America rose tenfold from 1700 to 1820, and by less than half in Mexico. Economic enterprise in North America was much more *dynamic* when the market was expanding so rapidly.

The way forward

Obviously, the conditions for sustained economic growth were not favorable in Latin America. However, most of these countries had gained independence almost two centuries ago, which is a long time during which changes for the better could have been made. These have, by and large, not happened. Latin America is stagnating. There was a time (i.e., around the Second World War) when Argentina and Venezuela belonged to the ten richest countries in the world. Now their economies are in the doldrums. Apparently, the political and institutional framework in place to provide the *incentives* that fuel growth, were inadequate to sustain their erstwhile prosperous position.

One important factor that does promote growth is innovation. It was Joseph Schumpeter who first pointed to this vital ingredient of growth in a capitalist system, and he coined it *creative destruction*. William Baumol, the veteran Princeton economist, recently elaborated on the role played by innovation in economic growth. He says that if the capitalist system can be seen as a machine whose primary product is economic growth, one of the machine's components is the Rule of Law, particularly the protection and enforcement of (intellectual) property rights. And it is precisely this that motivates innovators by ensuring that they can gain a reward for their efforts. Baumol argues that there are entrepreneurs in every sort of political system: how they differ is whether or not they devote their energies to productive innovations that add to economic growth. And this depends on the right *incentives* provided by the economic system.

The great leap forward that did not happen

The rapid progress that quite a few Asian economies were able to make during the past half-century did not take place in Latin America. Worse still, based on the poor growth rates of the past decade, it would take this continent 250 years to double its income. I fear that sustained economic development can only be brought about if a new political elite, supported by a majority vote stands up, which will change the rules of the game and in turn provide the incentives for growth of the Latin American economies, and do away with corrupt practices that greatly frustrate any form of development and poverty reduction.

Notes

1 The "financing gap" hypothesis is based on the Harrod-Domar model. It goes as follows: In order to grow, a country requires a certain level of investment. Poor countries generate too few savings to finance this required level of investment. Hence, aid should fill the gap. The aid will thus help augment investments, and – in turn – these investments will lead to the required economic growth. However, practice has shown that aid was not always directed to investments, but instead to for instance emergency assistance, health outlays and consumption. Moreover, investments did not necessarily lead to growth. If Zambia had converted all the aid it received since 1960 to investment and all of that investment to growth, it would have had a per capita GDP of about $ 20,000 by the early 1990s. Instead, Zambia's per capita GDP in the early 1990s was lower than it had been in 1960, hovering under $500 (William Easterly, *Can Foreign Aid buy Growth*; Journal of Economic Perspectives, Vol. 17, No. 3, Summer 2003, p. 33).
All this would explain why most poor countries do not *take off*, let alone move towards the path of self-sustained growth, as projected by Walt Rostow in *The Stages of Economic Growth* (Cambridge: Cambridge University Press, 1971). For a compelling explanation of the above refer to William Easterly's *The Elusive Quest for Growth; Economists' Adventures and Misadventures in the Tropics* (Cambridge MA: The MIT Press, 2002), pp. 2-69.

2 Out of 117 countries with populations of more than half a million people, only 18 have been able to sustain growth exceeding industrial countries' growth and have narrowed their per capita income gap with these countries (*Economic Growth in the 1990s: Learning from a Decade of Reform*, p. 5)

3 According to UNCTAD's *World Investment Report 2004*, FDI in low and middle-income countries amounted to USD 147 billion in 2003. Total Official Development Assistance (ODA) in that same year amounted to USD 69 billion. The 2003 total was the highest ever, both in nominal and real terms, according to the *Final ODA Data for 2003* (Paris: OECD, 2003). It should be noted that FDI is benefiting a minority, well performing middle-income countries. Most low-income countries depend on ODA for their investments. Moreover, FDI is highly volatile.
As for the importance of foreign direct investment Hansen and Tarp say: "Foreign direct investment, by itself, has a considerable impact on growth. This is partly because FDI is very sensitive to the policy regime and the institutional quality in the host country, and partly because FDI is an important vehicle for technology transfers". Henrik Hansen and Finn Tarp, *Aid and Growth Regressions* (Journal of Development Economics, Vol. 64 (2001)), p. 563.

4 Peter Bauer, *Dissent on Development; Revised Edition* (Cambridge MA: Harvard University Press, 1976)

5 There was at the time a much closer international contact between socialists or *dirigists* on one hand and market-oriented economists on the other hand; a situation to which F.A. Hayek drew attention many years ago.

6 Peter Bauer, *From Subsistence to Exchange* (Princeton: Princeton University Press, 2000), p. 105.

7 Ibid., p. 6.

8 Deepak Lal, *The Poverty of Development Economics* (Cambridge MA, The MIT Press, 2000), p. 5.

9 Ibid., p. 56.

10 In the Preface of the paperback edition of the *Elusive Quest for Growth* he wrote: "... the World Bank ...encourages gadflies like me to find another job."

11 Ibid., p. xii.

12 A pioneer in the study of incentives is Douglass North, whose work – strangely enough – is not mentioned by Easterly. North noted that disincentives can persist in the absence of efficient property rights. High transaction costs and the inefficiency of political markets can produce property rights that do not induce economic growth. These property rights can, moreover, result in the creation of new organizations, designed to prosper under existing laws which consequently have no incentive to create more efficient economic rules. Private gain is then made at the cost of overall economic growth. This description is, I believe, characteristic for quite a few developing countries. For more details on

North's thinking, see my essay on *The Institutional Dimension of Economic Growth*, pp. 111-131.

13 Easterly notes that even when economic performance is clearly deteriorating despite rising aid, as in the case of Africa during the past thirty years, the aid bureaucracies promise their constituencies – and themselves – that better times are "just around the corner" (*Can Foreign Aid Buy Growth?*), p. 35.

14 Charles Kenny and David Williams also reached this conclusion in their analysis of economic growth models. They conclude: "The practice of development has relied upon theories which purported to explain why developing countries had not experienced economic growth, and purported to be able to offer cogent advice on what should be done to overcome this. Yet the available evidence suggests that none of these theories has so far been able to do this very well (even when playing the far easier game of explaining past growth rather than improving future growth)", in: *What Do We Know about Economic Growth? Or, Why Don't We Know Very Much?* (World Development, Vol. 29, No. 1, 2000), p. 15.

15 *Can Foreign Aid Buy Growth?*, p. 40.

16 William Easterly, *The Cartel of Good Intentions: The Problem of Bureaucracy in Foreign Aid* (Policy Reform, Vol. 00, 2003), pp. 1-28.

17 For more details, refer to *Will World Poverty be Halved by 2015?*, pp. 156-160.

18 Center for Global Development, Working Paper number 44, revised version 2004.

19 Keith Griffin, *Foreign Capital, Domestic Savings, and Economic Development* (Bulletin of the Oxford University Institute of Economics and Statistics, 32 (2): pp. 99-112.

20 Gustav Papanek, *The Effects of Aid and other Resource Transfers on Savings and Growth in Less Developed Countries*, (Economic Journal 82 (327), 1972), pp. 934-950.

21 Paul Mosley, *Aid, Savings, and Growth Revisited* (Oxford Bulletin of Economics and Statistics 42 (2), 1980), pp. 79-96.

22 For further details refer to Clemens et al. p. 6.

23 Peter Boone, *Policies and the Effectiveness of Foreign Aid* (European Economic Review, 40 (2)), pp. 289-329.

24 Craig Burnside, David Dollar, *Aid, Policies and Growth* (American Economic Review, 40 (2)), pp. 289-329.

25 This prompts the urgent question of what to do about (near) failed states. I would say that also in this case prevention is better than the cure, as failed states breed violence and a fertile soil for terrorism.

26 Henrik Hansen & Finn Tarp, *Aid and Growth Regressions* (Journal of Development Economics Vol. 64, 2001), pp. 547-570.

27 Ibid., p. 566.

28 As for long-run effects the authors state: "We neither can nor endeavor to make any statements about the long-run effects of aid whose expected effect comes in the long run", *Counting the Chickens When they Hatch*, p. 12.

29 Hansen and Tarp draw a similar conclusion: "...aid in all likelihood increases the growth rate, and this result is not conditional on 'good' policy", *Aid and Growth Regressions*, p. 547.

30 NBER Working Paper Series, National Bureau of Economic Research (Cambridge, MA, July 2003).

31 *Aid, Policies and Growth: Revisiting the Evidence* (Washington DC: World Bank Policy Research Working Paper 3251, March 2004).

32 Raghuram Rajan and Arvind Subramanian, *Aid and Growth: What Does the Cross-Country Evidence Really Show?* (Washington DC: IMF Working Paper, June 2005)

33 Raghuram Rajan and Arvind Subramanian, *What Undermines Aid's Impact on Growth?* (Washington DC: IMF Working Paper, June 2005).

34 David Roodman, *The Anarchy of Numbers: Aid, Development, and Cross-country Empirics* (Center for Global Development, Working Paper No. 32, July 2004).

35 Ibid., p. 53.

36 *The Cartel of Good Intentions*, p. 25.

37 Nancy Birdsall, Dani Rodrik, Arvind Subramanian, *How to Help Poor Countries* (Foreign Affairs, July/August 2005) pp. 136-152.

38 World Bank, *Economic Growth in the 1990s: Learning from a Decade of Reform* (Washington DC, 2005).

39 *Economic Growth in the 1990s*, p. 25.

40 *Growth Strategies* (John F. Kennedy School of Management, Harvard University, August2004), *Rethinking Growth Policies in the Developing World* (Harvard University, October 2004).

41 Dani Rodrik, *Goodbye Washington Consensus, Hello Washington Confusion?* (Harvard University, January 2006).

42 This is confirmed by *Economic Growth in the 1990s*, which states on p. 6 that it is economic incentives which influence the evolution of institutions.

43 Ricardo Hausmann, Dani Rodrik, Andres Velasco, *Growth Diagnostics* (John F. Kennedy School of Government, Harvard University, March 2005).

44 Paul Collier, Jan Dehn, *Aid, Shocks, and Growth* (Policy Research Working Paper 2688, The World Bank Development Research Group, October 2001).

45 Ricardo Hausmann, Lant Pritchett, Dani Rodrik, *Growth Accelerations* (NBER Working Paper Series, Working Paper 10566, June 2004).

46 *The Cartel of Good Intentions*, p. 10.

47 Refer the graph concerned as presented in Easterly's *Can Foreign Aid Buy Growth*, p. 35.

48 Edward Glaeser, Rafael La Porta, Florencio Lopez-de-Salinas, Andrei Shleifer, *Do Institutions Cause Growth?* (NBER Working Paper Series, Working Paper 10568, June 2004). The authors say that economic growth will lead to institutional improvements in course of time.

49 Orhan Pamuk, *The Anger of the Damned* (The New York Review of Books, November 15, 2001), p. 12.

50 Stanley Hoffmann, *Clash of Globalizations* (Foreign Affairs, July/August 2002), pp. 107-108.

51 Martin Wolf, *Why Globalization Works* (New Haven and London, Yale University Press, 2004), p. 10.

52 Jagdish Bhagwati, *In Defense of Globalization* (New York, Oxford University Press, 2004), p. 3.

53 Thomas Friedman, *The Lexus and the Olive Tree* (New York, Anchor Books, 2000), p. ix.

54 *In Defense of Globalization*, p. 273.

55 "The exploitation of the world market has given a cosmopolitan character to production and consumption in every country. ...All old-established national industries have been destroyed or are daily being destroyed. They are dislodged by new industries, whose introduction becomes a life and death question for all civilized nations".

56 The time span of the first wave is the subject of different opinions. Jeffrey Williamson, for example, classifies the period 1820-1914 as the first great globalization era. (J. Williamson, *Winners and Losers over Two Centuries of Globalization*, NBER Working Paper, no. 9161, 2002).

57 *Globalization, Growth and Poverty, Building an Inclusive World Economy* (Washington DC, A World Bank Policy Research Report, January 2002), p. 5.

58 The accelerated growth of recent globalizers is consistent with other cross-country statistical analyses that find that trade goes hand-in-hand with faster growth. The most that these studies can establish is that more trade is correlated with higher growth, and one must be careful about drawing conclusions on causality. Some analysts say that even though no one study can establish that openness to trade has unambiguously helped the representative Third World economy, the preponderance of evidence supports this conclusion.

59 *Globalization, Growth, and Poverty*, p. 6.

60 The Economist, A Survey of India and China *The Tiger in Front*; 5 March 2005, p. 6.

61 As to why they missed the boat, there are various schools of thought. They can be grouped under the following views: (i) "Join the club" (ii) "Geographic disadvantage" and (iii) "Missed the boat" view. For further details see: *Globalization, Growth, and Poverty*, pp. 39-40.

62 Regarding poverty refer: *Will World Poverty be Halved by 2015?*, on pp. 156-160.

63 The World Bank, *Global Economic Prospects and the Developing Countries* (Washington DC, 2002), pp. 166-176.

64 *Why Globalization Works*, Chapter 10: *Traumatized by Trade*, pp. 173-219.

65 *Why Globalization Works*, p. 175.

66 Ibid.; p. 178-179.

67 Bjorn Lomborg, *The Skeptical Environmentalist: Measuring the Real State of the World* (Cambridge: Cambridge University Press, 2001), provides many examples.

68 John Cavenaugh, and others, *Alternatives to Globalization: A Better World is Possible*, Report of the International Forum on Globalization (San Francisco: Berrett-Koehler, 2002), p. 120.

69 Ha-Joon Chang, *Kicking Away the Ladder; Development Strategy in Historical Perspective* (London: Anthem Press, 2002).

70 Dani Rodrik, *The New Global Economy: Making Openness Work*, Policy Essay No. 24, (Baltimore: Johns Hopkins University Press, 1998).

71 Carlos Toranzo, et.al., *Bolivia en el Siglo XX; La Formación de Bolivia Contemporanéa* (La Paz, 1999), pp. 38-39.

72 Progressive Policy Institute, *America's Hidden Tax on the Poor: The Case for Reforming US Tariff Policy* (Washington DC, March 2002), pp. 10-12.

73 It should be noted that most poor countries are net importers of agricultural goods; 33 of the 49 poorest countries import more farm goods than they export; 45 of them are net importers of food. Subsidies depress the price of agricultural products on world markets. That obviously hurts rival exporters. But importers gain!

74 Joseph Stiglitz, *Globalization and its Discontent*, p. 245.

75 Geoffrey Garrett, *Globalization's Missing Middle* (Foreign Affairs, November/December 2004), pp. 84-96.

76 Amy Chua, *World on Fire; How Exporting Free Market Democracy Breeds Ethnic Hatred and Global Instability* (New York; Anchor Books, 2004).

77 *Why Globalization Works*, p. 314.

78 *World on Fire*, p. 124.

79 Ibid. p. 17.

80 Terrorism cannot only be the result of a lack of globalization, it can also be a threat to globalization. Niall Ferguson considers terrorism, supported by rogue states such as Iran and Syria, one of five threats to globalization as described by him in: *Sinking Globalization* (Foreign Affairs, March/April 2005), pp. 64-76.

81 This notion is very much inspired by Max Weber's classical definition of the state: "A territorially defined organization that successfully upholds a claim to the monopoly of the legitimate use of physical force in the enforcement of its orders", in Joseph F. Stiglitz et al., *The Economic Role of the State* (Oxford: Basil Blackwell, 1989), p. 21.

82 In Deepak Lal's *The Poverty of Development Economics* (Cambridge MA: The MIT Press, 2000) six phases are distinguished in the evolution of the global economy, influenced by economic policies. For a brief description, refer to Annex I.

83 Timothy Taylor provided a good description of the term "Globalization" in *The Public Interest*: "Globalization is not a magic cure-all for what ails a nation's economy, nor is it a plot by profit-hungry mega-corporations to exploit workers and spoil the environment. Globalization is not the return of colonialism, nor is it the arrival of world government. At the most fundamental level globalization simply means an expansion of the range of possible commercial activities. Seeking out and sorting through the possibilities opened up by globalization will require a daunting amount of effort, flexibility, and change, precisely because globalization embodies such a vast and marvelous array of new economic opportunities".

84 The Economist, *The Future of the State* (20 September 1997).

85 Jorge G. Castañeda, *The Forgotten Relationship, Rethinking US-Latin American Ties* (Foreign Affairs, May/June 2003).

86 For a resume of Plato's philosophy on the state, refer to Annex II.

87 Deepak Lal, *The Poverty of Development Economics*, p. 5

88 Michael Oakeshott, *On Human Conduct* (Oxford: Clarendon Press, 1975); *Morality and Politics in Modern Europe* (New Haven, Conn.: Yale University, 1993).

89 What follows, including economic data, is mainly based upon a survey entitled: *The Future of the State* (The Economist, September 1997).

90 In 2002 Singapore's economy shrank by 2 percent. This year's growth prognosis has been scaled down by the Singaporese authorities to 2 percent.

91 Martin Wolf, *Will the Nation-State Survive Globalization?* (Foreign Affairs, Jan/Feb. 2001).

92 Amartya Sen, *Development as Freedom* (New York: Anchor Books, 1999), p. 6.

93 *The Poverty of Development Economics*, p. 108

94 Peter Bauer, *Equality, the Third World and Economic Delusion* (London: Weidenfeld &Nicolson, 1987).

95 Merilee Grindle, *Challenging the State* (Cambridge University Press, 1996).

96 For a more detailed description of the NIE, refer my essay on *The Institutional Dimension of Economic Growth*, pp. 111-131.

97 *Challenging the State*, p. 7

98 To what extent, Grindle wonders, were there efforts by state elites and political institutions: "To reassert institutional capacity by defining and negotiating new rules of the game to govern economic and political behavior and forging new institutional structures and asserting their predominance over prior rules of behavior? To take advantage of increased technical capacity by developing and implementing alternative strategies for economic development, increasing the insulation of

economic policy making from domestic rent-seekers, or altering the policies that shape the behavior of economic interests in society? To compensate for weakened administrative capacity by experimenting with alternative production and service delivery mechanisms, introducing effective programs to compensate for the social costs of adjustment, or increasing public sector efficiency? To increase political capacity to mediate and resolve conflict and respond to societal demands by enhancing the problem-solving skills of government, incorporating new groups into decision making, allowing for increased political participation and local level problem-solving, and finding ways to increase technical input into decision making without compromising opportunities for wider participation?", ibid., p. 12.

99 William Baumol, *Entrepreneurship: Productive, Unproductive, and Destructive* (Journal of Political Economy; volume 98; Number 5, part 1; October 1990).

100 Baumol suggests that the five entrepreneurial activities as identified by Schumpeter in explaining growth, should be expanded by innovations in, for example, rent-seeking and the discovery of previously unused legal gambit that is effective in diverting rents to those who are first in exploiting it, leading to unproductive entrepreneurship.

101 Moses Finley, *Technical Innovation and Economic Progress in the Ancient World* (Econ. History Review, 18 August 1965), pp. 29-45.

102 Ibid., p. 39.

103 Etienne Balazs, *Chinese Civilization and Bureaucracy: Variations on a Theme* (New Haven: Yale University Press; 1964), p. 10.

104 This annex is quoted from: Deepak Lal, *The Poverty of Development Economics*, pp. 129-130.

105 What is written about Plato is based upon: *The Republic*; introduction by Desmond Lee (Hammondsworth: Penguin Classics, 1987).

106 Karl Popper, *The Open Society and its Enemies, Volume I Plato* (London: Routledge, 1977).

107 It appears that sex was in vogue at that time, not only in circles of psychoanalysts, but also amongst anthropologists such as Bronislaw Malinowsky, who published in 1929 *The Sexual Life of Savages in North-Western Melanesia*. The Preface was written by Havelock Ellis, author of the famous seven volumes *Studies in the Psychology of Sex*, reprinted in 1993.

108 "During the Sixteenth century, the highest developed countries (at that time China, the Andean countries, Mexico, and Mali) were 1.5 times richer than the rest of the world. Now, the gap between rich and poor is 80 times. During a large part of history – and for the majority of the societies in the past and present – the economic activities have been less than satisfactory. Human beings have, by trial and error, learned how to make economies perform better; but not only has this learning taken ten millennia (since the first economic revolution), it has still escaped the grasp of almost half the world's population. Moreover, the radical improvement of economic performance, even when narrowly defined as material well-being, is a modern phenomenon of the last few centuries and confined until the last few decades to a small part of the world'. This is what Douglass North said about economic development and stagnation in his Nobel Prize acceptance lecture on 9 December 1993.

109 Douglass North, *Structure and Change in Economic History* (New York: Norton, 1981), p. X.

110 *Mas Alla del Consenso de Washington; La Hora de la Reforma Institucional* (Washington DC: World Bank, 1998).

111 John Wallis & Douglass North, *Measuring the Transaction Sector in the American Economy*, In: Stanley Engerman &Robert Gallman, ed., *Long Term Factors in the Growth of the American Economy* (Chicago: Chicago University Press, 1986), pp. 95-148.

112 Deepak Lal, *Institutional Development and Economic Growth*, In: M. Oosterbaan, Th. de Ruyter van Steveninck, N. van der Windt, ed., *The Determinants of Economic Growth*, (Boston: Kluwer Academic Publishers, 2000), p. 167.

113 Robert Bates, *Social Dilemmas and Rational Individuals*, In: J. Harriss, J. Hunter and C. Lewis, *The New Institutional Economics and the Development of the Third World* (London: Routledge, 1995), p. 47.

114 Joel Mokyr, *The Handle of Richess* (New York: Oxford University Press, 1990).

115 I trust that the theories of Smith and Marx are well known. For this reason I only reflect the essence of Toynbee's grand theory, as contained in his *A Study of History*. It is based on the comparative analysis of 23 advanced civilizations. Evolution is explained as a system of

challenges and responses. However, evolution is not linear. Societies emerge, develop, and blossom, followed by a period of decay. Societal development thus follows a biological path, according to Toynbee. He wanted to derive lessons for Western society to help prevent its decay. In his later work Toynbee interprets the breakdown of societies as an opportunity to approach the ultimate objective of societies, namely to live in unity as God had intended. Toynbee projected a universal society that would act as a reflection of what God had meant for mankind. Tragically enough, when Toynbee reached these insights, he had clearly left the field of science and entered that of religion.

116   Adam Smith, *The Wealth of Nations* (New York: Modern Library, 1937) p. 538-539.
117   Philip Keefer, Stephan Knack, *Why don't Poor Countries Catch Up?* A Cross-National Test of an Institutional Explanation, (Economic Enquire, Vol. XXXXV, July 1997), pp. 590-602.
118   A vital condition for *catching up* in the neo-classical theory; hence this factor will delay catching up by deterring investment.
119   *Why don't Poor Countries Catch Up?*, p. 592.
120   K&K employ several measures of institutional quality and the security of property and contractual rights. Two independent international investor risk services (i) The International Country Risk Guide, and (ii) Business Environmental Risk Intelligence, separately evaluate such dimensions of institutional quality as bureaucratic quality and corruption. They also evaluate the quality of institutional outputs that bear on the security of property rights such as the Rule of Law, the risk of appropriation, and contract enforcebility.
121   Stephen Haber, ed., *Political Economy and Economic Growth in Latin America* (Stanford: Hoover Institution Press, 2000).
122   Ibid., pp. 282-283.
123   Robert Barro, *Determinants of Economic Growth* (Cambridge: Harvard University, 1996).
124   Mancur Olson, *Big Bills Left on the Sidewalk: Why Some Nations are Rich and Others Poor* (Journal of Economic Perspectives, 10 (2), 1996), pp. 3-24.
125   Ibid., p. 19.
126   *Institutions, Institutional Change and Economic Performance*, p. 117.
127   Jared Diamond, *Guns, Germs and Steel* (London: Vintage, 1998), p. 25.
128   Ibid., p. 68.
129   David Landes, *The Wealth and Poverty of Nations* (New York: Norton, 1998).
130   Ibid., p. 513.
131   *Institutions, Institutional Change and Economic Performance*, p. 140.
132   Douglass North, *Needed: A Theory of Change*, In: G. Meier and J. E. Stiglitz, ed., *Frontiers of Development Economics, The Future in Perspective* (Washington, Oxford University Press, 2001), p. 491.
133   E. Glaeser, R. La Porta, F. Lopez-de-Salines, A. Shleifer, *Do Institutions Cause Growth?* (National Bureau of Economic Research, Cambridge, MA, June 2004).
134   Seymour Lipset, *Political Man: The Social Basis of Modern Politics* (New York: Doubleday, 1960).
135   *Do Institutions Cause Growth?*, p. 3-4.
136   Refer to pp. 111-131.
137   Gerald Meier and Joseph Stiglitz, ed.: *Frontiers of Development Economics: The Future in Perspective* (Washington: Oxford University Press, 2001)
138   W. Arthur Lewis, who wrote the classic *The Theory of Economic Growth*, began lecturing on development economics at the University of Manchester in 1950. Before that, i.e., in 1947, he was appointed Reader in colonial economics at the University of London. The first seminar on development at the University of Oxford was offered by Hla Myint, also in 1950. The subject was introduced at Harvard and Yale in 1952-3.
139   Gerald Meier, *The Old Generation of Development Economists and the New*, In: *Frontiers of Development Economics*, pp. 13-50.
140   The Harrod-Domar equation is based on the crucial assumption that there is equilibrium between demand and supply of current output.
141   An erroneous advice. Gunnar Myrdal characterized the typical developing country state as "soft", hence, incapable of playing its role properly. It must be emphasized, though, that the models implied too many tasks for nascent government institutions. Arthur Lewis said this about it in his *Principles of Economic Planning*: "The government has too many tasks which can in advanced countries be left to entrepreneurs", p. 128.
142   Deepak Lal said about this in *The Poverty of Development Economics* (2000): "The most

important change in thinking in economic policy in the Third World has been the recognition that the assumptions about the nature of the state that underpinned planning are unrealistic. It was implicitly assumed that the state was benevolent, omniscient and omnipotent", p. 148.

143 The ideological contrast between, for example, the *Economic Commission for Latin America* (Prebisch et al.) and the World Bank doctrine became remarkable.

144 Paul Romer, *Idea Gaps and Object Gaps in Economic Development* (Journal of Monetary Economics, 32. December 1993), pp. 543-573.

145 Armatya Sen, *Development as Freedom* (New York: Anchor Books, 1999).

146 Lawrence Summers, *Research Challenges for Development Economics* (Finance and Development, 28; 3 September 1991), p. 5.

147 Paul Collier, *Social Capital and Poverty* (World Bank Social Capital Initiative Working Paper 4, 1998).

148 Gerald Meier, *The Old Generation of Development Economists and The New*, p. 33. Note: I wonder whether these institutions do have the capacities (think only of the trillions of dollars moving about daily in the international financial markets) and power (i.e., limited sanction possibilities) to achieve what Meier proposes. For the time being, the best bet would be strong capable Nation-States that can benefit from globalization whilst mitigating its threats.

149 Deepak Lal, *The Poverty of Development Economics*, p. 150.

150 On the question of the likelihood of an all encompassing theory of development, Deepak Lal observes in *The Poverty of Development Economics*: "...the type of speculations and research on the grand themes of culture and development, undertaken by 19th century social scientists like de Tocqueville and Max Weber, has sadly atrophied. A revival of this grand tradition is a precondition for thinking sensibly about these unsettled questions concerning economic transformation and development", p. 167.

151 Ted Galen Carpenter, *Bad Neighbor Policy; Washington's Futile War on Drugs in Latin America* (Palgrave, Mc Millan, Washington), 2003.

152 Paris: Development Centre of the Organization for Economic Co-operation and Development, 2001.